Meditation Prayer & Affirmations

Meditation Prayer & Affirmations

By Edgar Cayce

A.R.E. Press • Virginia Beach • Virginia

Contents

Contents

●

Foreword
Who Was Edgar Cayce?

Edgar Cayce (1877–1945) has been called "the Sleeping Prophet," "the father of holistic medicine," "the miracle man of Virginia Beach," and "the most documented psychic of all time." For forty-three years of his adult life, he had the ability to put himself into some kind of self-induced sleep state by lying down on a couch, closing his eyes, and folding his hands over his stomach. This state of relaxation and meditation enabled him to place his mind in contact with all time and space and gave him the ability to respond to any question he was asked. His responses came to be called "readings" and contain insights so valuable that even to this day Edgar Cayce's work is known throughout the world. Hundreds of books have explored his amazing psychic gift, and the entire range of Cayce material is accessed by tens of thousands of people daily via the Internet.

Although the vast majority of the Cayce material deals with health and every manner of illness, countless topics were explored using Cayce's psychic talent: dreams, philosophy, intuition, business advice, the Bible, education, child rearing, ancient civilizations, personal spirituality, human relationships, and much more. In fact, during Cayce's lifetime, he discussed an amazing 10,000 different subjects!

The Cayce legacy presents a body of information so valuable that Edgar Cayce himself might have hesitated to predict its impact on contemporary society. Who could have known that eventually terms such as *meditation, auras, spiritual growth, reincarnation,* and *holism* would become household words to millions? Edgar Cayce's A.R.E. (the Association for Research and Enlightenment, Inc.) has grown from its humble beginnings to an association with Edgar Cayce Centers in countries around the world. Today, the Cayce organizations are involved with hundreds of educational activities and outreach programs, children's camps, a multi-million dollar publishing company, membership benefits and services, volunteer contacts and programs worldwide, massage and health services, prison and prayer outreach programs, conferences and workshops, and affiliated schools (Atlantic University and the Cayce/Reilly School of Massotherapy).

Edgar Cayce was born and reared on a farm near Hopkinsville, Kentucky. He had a normal childhood in many respects. However, he could see the glowing energy patterns that surround individuals. At a very early age he also told his parents that he could see and talk with his grandfather—who was deceased. Later, he developed the ability to sleep on his schoolbooks and retain a photographic memory of their entire contents.

As the years passed, he met and fell in love with Gertrude Evans, who would become his wife. Shortly thereafter, he developed a paralysis of the vocal cords and could scarcely speak above a whisper. Everything was tried, but no physician was able to locate a cause. The laryngitis persisted for months. As a last resort, hypnosis was tried. Cayce put himself to sleep and was asked by a specialist to describe the problem. While asleep, he spoke normally, diagnosing the ailment and prescribing a simple treatment. After the recommendations were followed, Edgar Cayce could speak normally for the first time in almost a year! The date was March 31, 1901—that was the first reading.

When it was discovered what had happened, many others began to want help. It was soon learned that Edgar Cayce could put himself into this unconscious state and give readings for anyone—regardless of where they were. If the advice was followed, they got well. Newspapers throughout the country carried articles about his work, but it wasn't really until Gertrude was stricken with tuberculosis that the readings were brought home to him. Even with medical treatments she continued to grow worse and was not expected to live. Finally, the doctors said there was nothing more they could do. A reading was given, and it recommended osteopathy, inhalants, enemas, dietary changes, and prescription medication. The advice was followed, and Gertrude returned to perfectly normal health! For decades, the Cayce readings have stood the test of time, research, and extensive study. Further details of Cayce's life and work are explored in such classic books as *There is a River* (1942) by Thomas Sugrue, *The Sleeping Prophet* (1967) by Jess Stearn, *Many Mansions* (1950) by Gina Cerminara, and *Edgar Cayce: An American Prophet* (2000) by Sidney Kirkpatrick. Further information about Edgar Cayce's A.R.E., as well as activities, materials, and services, is available at www.EdgarCayce.org.

Throughout his life, Edgar Cayce claimed no special abilities, nor did he ever consider himself to be some kind of twentieth-century prophet. The readings never offered a set of beliefs that had to be embraced but instead focused on the fact that each person should test in his or her own life the principles presented. Though Cayce himself was a Christian and read the Bible from cover to cover every year of his life, his work was one that stressed the importance of comparative study among belief systems all over the world. The underlying principle of the readings is the oneness of all life, a tolerance for all people, and a compassion and understanding for every major religion in the world.

An Overview of Edgar Cayce on "Meditation, Prayer and Affirmations"

The Edgar Cayce information on meditation, prayer and affirmations has touched the lives of hundreds of thousands of individuals around the world. To be sure, Cayce was one of the first sources in the Western Hemisphere to consistently recommend meditation to individuals from every religious background. The Cayce readings on prayer advance the ecumenical nature of prayer and discuss the workings and vibrations of this integral tool for personal attunement and spiritual healing. In terms of affirmations, the Cayce material frequently extols the extraordinary power of the "mind as the builder" and the premise that personal co-creation is empowered by that which the mind dwells upon. In other words, what one continues to think, one eventually becomes. With all of this in mind, it is perhaps ironic that this extremely invaluable wealth of information grew out of personal failure on the part of Edgar Cayce.

As brief background information, approximately two-thirds of the Cayce readings deal with health and the treatment of physical illness and disease. Edgar Cayce's lifelong dream was to have a hospital where individuals could come and receive psychic readings from him and where physicians and health care professionals from every discipline and background could carry out the recommended treatments. The readings are a strong proponent of people in every school of medicine learning how to cooperate and coexist for the ultimate benefit of the patient.

For decades, Edgar Cayce sought funding for his hospital before finally receive support from two New York businessmen brothers who financed the Edgar Cayce Hospital in Virginia Beach, Virginia (the location recommended by the readings). The hospital opened in 1928, and Cayce's dream became a reality. The dream was short-lived, however, and the hospital was lost in 1931 during the Depression. Edgar Cayce was devastated. He was 54 years old, and it appeared that his purpose for living was over.

In response to the hospital's failure and in an effort to find another focus for Cayce's amazing psychic talent, a group of Cayce's friends rallied around him looking for a way to work with the readings as a group. Some of the individuals were interested in obtaining readings on how they could become more psychic themselves. Others hoped to learn how to become more spiritual, helping their families and the world at large in the process. Edgar Cayce's readings to the group presented the unique idea that psychic development was actually a natural by-product of spiritual growth and attunement. It was for this reason that the group began receiving a series of readings that promised "light to a waiting world."

None of the original group members could have imagined the impact their meetings would have upon the rest of their lives nor upon the lives of countless others even decades later. The group called themselves a study group, and group members worked for years to compile two books on lessons in spiritual growth that would eventually be published as *A Search for God*, Books I & II.[1]

The group activity gave birth to much more than material on soul growth and personal transformation. After the first meeting, Edgar Cayce had a dream that led to the formation of a prayer group made up of some of the original study group members. This group called itself the Glad Helpers Prayer Group[2], and it was specifically interested in the possibility of group members raising personal vibration and consciousness as a means of becoming healing channels to others through prayer

---

[1&2] Note: Both the Study Group and the Prayer Group activities of Edgar Cayce's A.R.E. continue to this day. Visit www.EdgarCayce.org for additional information.

and spiritual healing. Essentially, the premise of the readings on meditation, prayer, and attunement is that as an individual raises his or her personal consciousness, spiritual healing can be directed to others "on the wings of thought." In addition to having ongoing meetings, the group would receive sixty-five readings on topics including meditation, prayer, the use of affirmations, consciousness development, vibrations, and even a series of readings on interpreting the Book of Revelation.

Although we may think of prayer as telling God what we need or want, Cayce believed that true prayer was not so much a petition for things as it was an expression of one's desire to gain an awareness of the Creator's will in our lives. In other words, prayer invites God to work through us. Meditation, on the other hand, is clearing aside all random thoughts so that we might become more attuned to the Divine. In the language of the readings, both are explained as follows:

Reading 1861-19[3]

For prayer is supplication for direction, for understanding. Meditation is listening to the Divine within.

Reading 5368-1

Then set definite periods for prayer; set definite periods for meditation. Know the difference between each. Prayer, in short, is appealing to the divine within self, the divine from without self, and meditation is keeping still in body, in mind, in heart, listening, listening to the voice of thy Maker.

Although some schools of thought contend that the mind gets in the way of the meditator and must therefore be blanked out, the Cayce information suggests that whatever the mind focuses upon becomes a greater portion of the individual's core: physically, mentally, and spiritually. In fact, when used constructively, the mind is a powerful tool that allows for a greater sense of relaxation and an awareness of the

---

[3]The Edgar Cayce readings are numbered to maintain confidentiality. The first set of numbers (e.g., "1861") refers to the individual or group for whom the reading was given. The second set of numbers (e.g., "19") refers to the number of the reading for that individual or group.

closest possible attunement. For that reason, the readings recommend using affirmations while meditating.

In addition to the importance of the mind's focus, Cayce also stated that an individual's *ideal* or intent was extremely important during the practice of meditation. Ultimately, the purpose of meditation should be centered around the concept of learning how to better express divine love in our interactions with one another. Actually, the readings suggested that the entire process of meditation should be taken seriously, as it was one of the best vehicles for cultivating our personal relationship with the Divine:

Reading 281–41

Purify thy body. Shut thyself away from the cares of the world. Think on that as ye would do to have thy God meet thee face to face. "Ah," ye say "but many are not able to speak to God!" Many, you say, are fearful. Why? Have ye gone so far astray that ye cannot approach Him who is all merciful? He knows thy desires and thy needs, and can only supply according to the purposes that ye would perform within thine own self. Then, purify thy body, physically. Sanctify thy body, as the laws were given of old, for tomorrow the Lord would speak with thee—as a father speaketh to his children . . . Know that thy body is the temple of the living God. *There* He has promised to meet thee!

Any individual can take advantage of Cayce's suggested approach to meditation by following a few simple steps. First, get into a comfortable position. It's probably best to sit in a chair, keeping your spine straight, your feet flat on the floor, and your eyes closed. Find a comfortable place for your hands, either in your lap or at your sides. In order to help with a balanced flow of energy throughout the physical body, keep your palms face down against your legs or closed against your stomach. Slowly take a few deep breaths and begin to relax. Breathe the air deeply into your lungs, hold it for a moment, and then slowly breathe it out. With your mind, search your body for any obvious tension or tight muscles. You can try to relieve the tension by deep breathing, imagining the area to be relaxed, or gently massaging any tightness with your fingertips. When you have become comfortable and more at ease than when you first sat down, you are ready to move on. You may wish to try a breathing exercise recommended in the Cayce readings to assist in even greater levels of relaxation and attunement. Very simply, it is as follows:

First, breathe in slowly through the right nostril (covering the left nostril with your hand and keeping the mouth closed), then pinch your nostrils and breathe out through the mouth. Repeat this for a total of three times. Second, with your mouth closed, slowly breathe in through the left nostril (covering the right), then cover the left and breathe out through the right. Repeat this, as well, for a total of three times.

When your breathing exercise is complete, next begin to focus your mind on a meditation affirmation or perhaps a single, peaceful, calming thought. Instead of thinking about what went on at work or what has to be accomplished with the remainder of your day, try focusing instead on a thought such as "I am at peace" or one of the many affirmations suggested by the readings. You can also use a biblical verse (such as the Twenty-third Psalm or the Lord's Prayer) or a thought with a focus such as "God is Love." Any of these focuses can be considered an affirmation.

The first stage of meditation involves thinking about the message of your affirmation. With one of the examples cited above, you would think about the words "I am at peace." After a few moments of thinking the words, you should be able to move onto the second stage of meditation, which is feeling the meaning behind those words. For example, you could continue saying the words "I am at peace," but the feeling behind these words can be much more meaningful than the actual words themselves. An analogy can reveal how a feeling is more all encompassing than a thought. Consider saying the words "I love my child" versus the feeling behind those words. From Cayce's perspective, whenever individuals are able to hold the feeling of the affirmation throughout their entire being, they are truly meditating and building the focus of the affirmation within themselves.

During this second stage of meditation, the individual should try to hold the feeling of the affirmation in silent attention without needing to repeat the words. Whenever the mind begins to wander, simply bring your focus back to the words of the affirmation. Once again you would begin by thinking the words of the affirmation and then by trying to concentrate on the feeling behind those words. Individuals shouldn't become discouraged if they find themselves thinking more about distractions than they are focusing upon the affirmation—it takes practice. To begin with, an individual might want to spend anywhere from three minutes to fifteen minutes trying to hold the affirmation silently. Longer meditation periods will become possible with practice and experience.

With regard to closing a meditation period, the readings emphasized the importance of consciously sending out prayers and good thoughts to other people and situations in life. At this point an individual may wish to open the palms to enable the energy of meditation to flow through them. Since we do not always know what may be best for an individual's personal growth and development, it is best to simply pray that the individual be surrounded by light, love, and God's will–presence and protection rather than praying for something specific. As we begin to practice meditation daily, it will become easier. We might also discover that whatever feeling we have been focusing upon in meditation will actually begin to carry over into greater portions of the day.

Sometimes certain physical sensations may occur in meditation: energy rising up the spine, gentle movements of the head and neck in a circular or side-to-side motion, etc. These sensations are simply a result of the movement of energy (often called the *kundalini* or even *spiritual energy*) rising through the endocrine centers of your body: gonads, leydig, adrenals, thymus, thyroid, pineal, and pituitary.

Through the regular practice of meditation, you can begin to heal yourself on many levels. As you focus upon a positive affirmation, you may find that your negative habit-patterns will begin to change to be more in keeping with your positive affirmation. It is while practicing the silence of meditation, by relaxing your physical body and by quieting your conscious mind, that you can set aside your daily concerns and attempt to attune yourself to your spiritual source.

Perhaps more than anything else, meditation, prayer, and the use of spiritual affirmations are tools for attunement, and personal attunement is at the core of understanding our true spiritual essence. In Cayce's worldview, the end result of soul development is that all individuals will eventually realize their true spiritual self and their connection to the whole. Actually, the readings told a thirty–six–year–old lawyer that this realization was the ultimate cause of each individual's creation in the first place:

Reading 826–11

What then is the purpose of the entity's activity in the consciousness of mind, matter, spirit in the present?

That it, the entity, may know itself to be itself and part of the Whole; not the Whole but one with the Whole; and thus retaining its individuality, knowing itself to be itself yet one with the purposes of the First Cause that called it, the entity into being, into the awareness, into the consciousness of itself.

For decades, individuals from every background and religious tradition have found the Edgar Cayce information on meditation, prayer, and affirmations extremely helpful in their own personal growth and attunement. This book of excerpts from the Cayce readings has been compiled to provide an understanding of meditation and prayer and the co–creative potential all individuals possess in coming to know themselves and their relationship with the Divine. With this in mind, it may be read for insights into personal attunement or even as a daily devotional. This is the approach to meditation, prayer, and affirmations that is found in the Edgar Cayce readings.

Kevin J. Todeschi
Executive Director & CEO
Edgar Cayce's A.R.E. / Atlantic University

1

●

General Insights on Meditation and Prayer

The Importance of Meditation

(Note: Because of the way in which this reading, given to the original prayer group, specifically addresses the overall topic of this chapter, it has been included in its entirety.)

TEXT OF READING 281-41

This psychic reading given by Edgar Cayce at the Hotel Warner, 34th & Ocean, Virginia Beach, Va., this 15th day of June, 1939, with forty present from outside Norfolk and Virginia Beach area. [The Reading was stenciled from GD's shorthand notes and mimeographed with this heading for use in the Eighth Annual Congress Booklet.] (When Book I, SFG was published in 1942 this reading was included in the chapter on Meditation.)

PRESENT

Edgar Cayce; Gertrude Cayce, Conductor; Gladys Davis, Steno. Hugh Lynn Cayce, and local members of groups, etc.

READING

Time of Reading 4:00 P. M.

GC: You will have before you those assembled here who seek information on meditation which will be helpful to them and others.

EC: In the mind of many there is little or no difference between meditation and prayer. And there are many gathered here who, through their studies of various forms, have very definite ideas as to meditation and prayer.

There are others that care not whether there be such things as meditation, but depend upon someone else to do their thinking, or are satisfied to allow circumstance to take its course—and hope that sometime, somewhere, conditions and circumstances will adjust themselves to such a way that the best that may be will be their lot.

Yet, to most of you, there must be something else—some desire, something that has prompted you in one manner or another to seek to be here now, that you may gather something from a word, from an act, that will either give thee hope or make thee better satisfied with thy present lot, or to *justify* thee in the course ye now pursue.

To each of you, then, we would give a word:

Ye all find yourselves confused at times respecting from whence ye came and whither ye goeth. Ye find yourselves with bodies, with minds—not all beautiful, not all clean, not all pure in thine own sight or in thy neighbor's. And there are many who care more for the outward appearance than that which prompts the heart in its activity or in its seeking.

But, ye ask, what has this to do with Meditation? What *is* Meditation?

It is not musing, not daydreaming; but as ye find your bodies made up of the physical, mental and spiritual, it is the attuning of the mental body and the physical body to its spiritual source.

Many say that ye have no consciousness of having a soul—yet the very fact that ye hope, that ye have a desire for better things, the very fact that ye are able to be sorry or glad, indicates an activity of the mind that takes hold upon something that is not temporal in its nature— something that passeth not away with the last breath that is drawn but that takes hold upon the very sources of its beginning—the *soul*—that which was made in the image of thy Maker—not thy body, no—not thy mind, but thy *soul* was in the image of thy Creator.

Then, it is the attuning of thy physical and mental attributes seeking to know the relationships to the Maker. *That* is true meditation.

How do you accomplish same? How would ye as an individual go about learning to meditate?

For, ye must learn to meditate—just as ye have learned to walk, to talk, to do any of the physical attributes of thy mind as compared to the relationships with the facts, the attitudes, the conditions, the environs of thy daily surroundings.

Then, there must be a conscious contact with that which is a part of thy body-physical, thy body-mental, to thy soul-body or thy superconsciousness. The names indicate that ye have given it metes and bounds, while the soul is boundless—and is represented by many means or measures or manners in the expressions in the mind of each of you.

But there are physical contacts which the anatomist finds not, or those who would look for imaginations or the minds. Yet it is found that within the body there are channels, there are ducts, there are glands, there are activities that perform no one knows what! in a living, *moving*, thinking being. In many individuals such become dormant. Many have become atrophied. Why? Non-usage, non-activity! because only the desires of the appetite, self-indulgences and such, have so glossed over or used up the abilities in these directions that they become only wastes as it were in the spiritual life of an individual who has so abused or misused those abilities that have been given him for the greater activity.

Then, purify thy mind if ye would meditate. How? Depending on what is thy concept of purification! Does it mean to thee a mixing up with a lot of other things, or a setting aside of self, a washing with water, a cleansing or purifying by fire or what not?

Whatever thy concept is, be *true* to thine inner self. *Live* that choice ye make—*do it!* not merely say it but *do it!*

Purify thy body. Shut thyself away from the cares of the world. Think on that as ye would do to have thy God meet thee face to face. "Ah," ye say "but many are not able to speak to God!" Many, you say, are fearful. Why? Have ye gone so far astray that ye cannot approach Him who is all merciful? He knows thy desires and thy needs, and can only supply according to the purposes that ye would perform within thine own self.

Then, purify thy body, physically. Sanctify thy body, as the laws were

given of old, for tomorrow the Lord would speak with thee—as a father
speaketh to his children. Has God changed? Have ye wandered so far
away? Know ye not that, as He has given, "If ye will be my children, I
will be thy God"? and "Though ye wander far away, if ye will but call I
will hear"?

If any of you say, "Yes, but it was spoken to those of old—we have no
part in such," then indeed ye have no part. They that would know God,
would know their own souls, would know how to meditate or to talk
with God, must believe that He *is*—and that He rewards those who seek
to know and to do His biddings.

That He gave of old is as new today as it was in the beginning of
man's relationship or seeking to know the will of God, if ye will but call
on Him *within* thine inner *self!* Know that thy body is the temple of the
living God. *There* He has promised to meet thee!

Are ye afraid? Are ye ashamed? Have ye so belittled thy opportunities, have ye so defamed thine own body and thine own mind that ye
are ashamed to have thy God meet thee within thine own tabernacle?

Then, woe be unto thee—lest ye set thy house in order. For as has
been indicated, there are physical contacts in thy own body with thy
own soul, thy own mind. Does anyone have to indicate to you that if
you touch a needle there is pain felt? Ye are told that such an awareness
is an activity of consciousness that passes along the nervous system to
and from the brain. Then, just the same there are contacts with that
which is eternal within thy physical body. For there is the bowl that
must one day be broken, the cord that must one day be severed from
thine own physical body—and to be absent from the body is to be
present with God.

What is thy God? Are thy ambitions only set in whether ye shall eat
tomorrow, or as to wherewithal ye shall be clothed? Ye of little faith, ye
of little hope, that allow such to become the paramount issues in thine
own consciousness! Know ye not that ye are His? For ye are of His
making! He hath willed that ye shall not perish, but hath left it with
thee as to whether ye become even aware of thy relationships with Him
or not. In thine own house, in thine own body there are the means for
the approach—through the desire first to know Him; putting that desire
into activity by purging the body, the mind of those things that ye

know or even conceive of as being hindrances—not what someone else says! It isn't what you want someone else to give! As Moses gave of old, it isn't who will descend from heaven to bring you a message, nor who would come from over the seas, but Lo, ye find Him within thine own heart, within thine own consciousness! if ye will *meditate*, open thy heart, thy mind! Let thy body and mind be channels that *ye* may *do* the things ye ask God to do for you! Thus ye come to know Him.

Would you ask God to do for you that you would not do for your brother? If you would, you are selfish—and know not God. For as ye do it unto the least of thy brethren, ye do it unto thy Maker. These are not mere words—they are that as ye will *experience*—if ye would know Him at all. For He is not past finding out; and if ye will know Him, tune in to Him; turn, look, hope, act in such a way that ye *expect* Him, thy God, to meet thee face to face. "Be not afraid, it is I," saith He that came to those seeking to know their relationship with their Maker. And because He came walking in the night, in the darkness, even upon the waters, they were afraid. Yea, many of you become afraid because of the things that ye hear—for ye say, "I do not *understand*—I do not *comprehend!*" Why? Have ye so belittled thyself, thy body, thy mind, thy consciousness, that thou hast seared, that thou hast made of none effect those opportunities within thine own consciousness to know thy Maker?

Then, to all of you:

Purify thy body, thy mind. Consecrate thyselves in prayer, yes—but not as he that prayed "I thank Thee I am not like other fellows." Rather let there be in thy heart that humbleness, for ye must humble thyself if ye would know Him; and come with an open, seeking, contrite heart, desirous of having the way shown to thee.

And when thou art shown, turn not thy face the other way; but be true to the vision that is given thee. And He will speak, for His promise has been "When ye call I will hear, and will answer speedily." Then, when He speaks, open thy heart, thy mind to the opportunities, to the glories that are thine—if ye will but accept them through that attuning through meditation of thy consciousness, thy desire to the *living* God; and say and live within thyself as He of old gave, "Others may do as they may, but as for me, I will worship—yea, I will serve the living God."

He is not far from thee! He is closer than thy right hand. He standeth at the door of thy heart! Will ye bid Him enter? or will ye turn away?

Additional Insights Given to the Original Prayer Group
Reading 281-13

When an individual then enters into deep meditation:

It has been found throughout the ages (*individuals* have found) that self-preparation (to *them*) is necessary. To some it is necessary that the body be cleansed with pure water, that certain types of breathing are taken, that there may be an even balance in the whole of the respiratory system, that the circulation becomes normal in its flow through the body, that certain or definite odors produce those conditions (or are conducive to producing of conditions) that allay or stimulate the activity of portions of the system, that the more carnal or more material sources are laid aside, or the whole of the body is *purified* so that the purity of thought as it rises has less to work against in its dissemination of that it brings to the whole of the system, in its rising through the whole of these centers, stations or places along the body. To be sure, these are conducive; as are also certain incantations, as a drone of certain sounds, as the tolling of certain tones, bells, cymbals, drums, or various kinds of skins. Though we may as higher thought individuals find some fault with those called savages, they produce or arouse or bring within themselves—just as we have known, do know, that there may be raised through the battle-cry, there may be raised through the using of certain words or things, the passion or the thirst for destructive forces. Just the same may there be raised, not sedative to these but a *cleansing* of the body.

"Consecrate yourselves this day that ye may on the morrow present yourselves before the Lord that He may speak through *you!*" is not amiss. So, to *all* there may be given:

Find that which is to *yourself* the more certain way to your consciousness of *purifying* body and mind, before ye attempt to enter into the meditation as to raise the image of that through which ye are seeking to know the will or the activity of the Creative Forces; for ye are *raising* in meditation actual *creation* taking place within the inner self!

When one has found that which to self cleanses the body, whether from the keeping away from certain foods or from certain associations (either man or woman), or from those thoughts and activities that would hinder that which is to be raised from *finding* its full measure of expression in the *inner* man (*inner* man, or inner individual, man or woman, meaning in this sense those radial senses from which, or centers from which all the physical organs, the mental organs, receive their stimuli for activity), we readily see how, then, *in* meditation (when one has so purified self) that *healing of every* kind and nature may be disseminated on the wings of thought, that are so much a thing—and so little considered by the tongue that speaks without taking into consideration what may be the end thereof!

Now, when one has cleansed self, in whatever manner it may be, there may be no fear that it will become so overpowering that it will cause any physical or mental disorder. It is *without* the cleansing that entering any such finds *any* type or form of disaster, or of pain, or of any dis-ease of any nature. It is when the thoughts, then, or when the cleansings of *group* meditations are conflicting that such meditations call on the higher forces raised within self for manifestations and bring those conditions that either draw one closer to another or make for that which shadows [shatters?] much in the experiences of others; hence short group meditations with a *central* thought around some individual idea, or either in words, incantations, or by following the speech of one sincere in abilities, efforts or desires to raise a cooperative activity *in* the minds, would be the better.

Then, as one formula—not the only one, to be sure—for an individual that would enter into meditation for self, for others:

Cleanse the body with pure water. Sit or lie in an easy position, without binding garments about the body. Breathe in through the right nostril three times, and exhale through the mouth. Breathe in three times through the left nostril and exhale through the right. Then, either with the aid of a low music, or the incantation of that which carries self deeper—deeper—to the seeing, feeling, experiencing of that image in the creative forces of love, enter into the Holy of Holies. As self feels or experiences the raising of this, see it disseminated through the *inner* eye (not the carnal eye) to that which will bring the greater understanding in meeting every condition in the experience of the body. Then listen to the music that is made as each center of thine own body responds to

that new creative force that little by little this entering in will enable self
to renew all that is necessary—in Him.

First, *cleanse* the room; cleanse the body; cleanse the surroundings, in
thought, in act! Approach not the inner man, or the inner self, with a
grudge or an unkind thought held against *any* man! or do so to thine
own undoing sooner or later!

Prayer and meditation:

Prayer is the concerted effort of the physical consciousness to become attuned to the consciousness of the Creator, either collectively or
individually! *meditation* is *emptying* self of all that hinders the creative
forces from rising along the natural channels of the physical man to be
disseminated through those centers and sources that create the activities of the physical, the mental, the spiritual man; properly done must
make one *stronger* mentally, physically, for has it not been given? He
went in the strength of that meat received for many days? Was it not
given by Him who has shown us the Way, "I have had meat that ye
know not of"? As we give out, so does the *whole* of man—physically and
mentally become depleted, yet in entering into the silence, entering
into the silence in meditation, with a clean hand, a clean body, a clean
mind, we may receive that strength and power that fits each individual,
each soul, for a greater activity in this material world.

"Be not afraid, it is I." Be sure it is Him we worship that we raise in our
inner selves for the dissemination; for, as He gave, "Ye must eat of my
body; ye must drink of *my* blood." Raising then in the inner self that
image of the Christ, love of the God–Consciousness, is *making* the body
so cleansed as to be barred against all powers that would in any manner hinder.

Be thou *clean*, in Him.

Reading 281–27

(Q) [540]: *Please interpret the experience I had on Friday night, May 29th, in
which I saw colors and heard a voice speak within me.*

(A) Much might be given as to colors, as to voice, as to the experience
that came to thee. As has been given, these experiences come as warn-
ings, as strength, as might, as power, that ye may be comforted in those
experiences that at times would overwhelm thee and make thee doubt

even thine own self. Know, then, that the lights, the voice, are as the power of the Christ in thine life, *attuning* thee that thou may be a greater help, a greater blessing to others; at the same time encouraging thee, lifting thee up to a more perfect knowledge of the glories of the Lord as He worketh in and through thee.

The lights are as the spirit of *truth;* the voice as the oneness with Him, that must be maintained if thy strength would maintain thee.

(Q) [585]: Please explain just what took place the night I heard what sounded like a large top spinning—felt a strong vibration sweep through my body and when I spoke saw a bluish spark close to the top of my head and it felt like electricity.

(A) As hath been indicated for the group, for members of same, there is that line, that connection, that point of contact in the body–physical to the spiritual forces as manifest through same. There are the centers of the body through which contacts are made, or are physically active, that at times, at all times, produce a sound. It may not be heard, it may not be always experienced by the individual, but finds expression in emotions of varied centers, varied characters. Thus the experience is that of the broader contact. Thus there are the vibrations of the electrical energies of the body, for Life itself is electrical—it manifests itself in its contacts in a physical being in much the same manner. Thus the experience in self of the emotions–physical being contacted by emotions–spiritual manifesting in the body.

These are, then, as experiences. Learn ye to use them, for they will give expressions in many ways and manners. Seek experiences not as experiences alone but as purposefulness. For what be the profit to thyself, to thy neighbor, if experiences alone of such natures rack thy body— owing to its high vibration—without being able to make thee a kinder mother, a more loving wife, a better neighbor, a better individual in every manner? *These* be the fruits, that it makes thee kinder, gentler, stronger in body, in mind, in purpose to *be* a channel through which the love of *God,* through Jesus Christ, may be manifested in the world. Not as a vision, an experience alone.

(Q) Why do I have such a feeling of fullness in my hands when I am holding my healing meditations?

(A) A natural consequence of that as has just been given. Pour it out, not hold it in self.

Reading 281-14

(Q) *Please expand on the different circular vibrations which are experienced during meditation: 1. When felt in the lower part of body.*

(A) As this may be expanded upon both from the metaphysical viewpoint and from the purely scientific also, well that those who experience these do not confuse themselves in the interpreting of that each may experience. Each must remember that the vibrations which are emanations of the Life from *within* are a material expression of a spiritual influence, or of a *force* that may *emanate* from Life itself.

Now, consider, we are viewing both of these in the light of that which has just been given.

When an emanation or a vibration arises, it may only act upon centers within the human body that are sensitive to those vibrations *within* the body; else one may not become aware of such vibrations being present, or they may not become apparent; hence have within themselves passed from being an influence that is not of a nature other than that which produced same.

When these *are* interpreted properly, they become that which raises for each individual the ability to become aware of the influences from without and from within. These, *spiritualized,* are the emanations that may be sent out as thought waves, as a force in the activity of universal or cosmic influence, and thus have their effect upon those to whom by suggestive force they are directed toward.

In the *varied* motions, as we understand, these arise; (as all things spiral *would*), for one that *would* become aware of such an emanation, such a vibration, such a force being active within themselves.

Do not use those vibrations to self's undoing, by the attempts to make for *self* other than a *channel* for aid to another.

(Q) *When felt in the lower part of the body.*

(A) All the same. We begin from one. We have passed on up to the head now!

(Q) [341]: *Please explain the sensations during meditation of vibration running up through the body and ending in a sort of fullness in the head.*

(A) The various portions, as given, represent the activities that are being set, either when considered from the purely scientific or from the metaphysical standpoint, as an active force emanating from the Life itself within. Then, these become all-embracing; hence the better understanding should be gained, whether used to disseminate and bring healing or for the raising of the forces in self. When one is able to so raise within themselves such vibrations, as to pass through the whole course of the attributes of physical attunements, to the disseminating force or center, or the Eye, then the body of that individual becomes a magnet that may (if properly used) bring healing to others with the laying on of hands. This is the manner in which such a healing becomes effective *by* the laying on of hands.

(Q) *Should one allow unconsciousness to follow?*

(A) Unconsciousness is a physical-natural consequence, unless there is the radiation passed off into some other force for raising same, or aiding same.

(Q) *How can one direct the vibration culminating in the head to the one they would aid?*

(A) By *thought.* (Now we are speaking of a purely mechanical, meta-physical-spiritual activity that would take place.) One has directed their thought to an individual who is to *receive* the blessing of that power or force raised. They raise within themselves that which may be sent out as a power, and it passes to those that would be in attune or accord. Were they present a much greater force may be felt, to be sure; less is the strain upon the physical body.

We are through for the present.

Reading 281-5

(Q) *While meditating have experienced a perfect relaxation of the body, the head being drawn backward. Please explain.*

(A) The nearer the body of an individual, or this, draws to that attunement, or consciousness, as was in the Christ Consciousness, as is in the Christ Consciousness, the nearer does the body, or that body, become a channel for *life—living* life—to others to whom the thought is directed. Hence at such periods, these are the manifestations of the life, or the spirit, acting *through* the body.

(Q) [993]: *On several occasions while meditating with the group there was a cool feeling as if mentholatum had been placed upon my head and forehead, extending down upon the nose.*

(A) As would be termed—literal—as the breath of an angel, or the breath of a master. As the body attunes self, as has been given, it may be a channel where there may be even *instant* healing with the laying on of hands. The more often this occurs the more *power* is there felt in the body, the forcefulness in the act or word.

(Q) *After meditating with the group on April 11th, my whole body seemed to be vibrating to the thought that I had opened my heart to the unseen forces that surround the throne of grace, and beauty, and might, and throwing about self that protection that is found in the thoughts of Him. Please explain.*

(A) Just as has been given, the nearer one—a body, this body—draws to that complete consciousness that is in Him, the greater may be the power—that is manifested through His presence in the world through that as is brought about in self's own experience. The more forceful, the more helpful, does the body become at such, and through such, experiences. Let these remain as sacred experiences, gathering more and more of same—but as such is given out, so does it come.

(Q) [341]: *How can I develop greater spiritual control over the mental body during meditations?*

(A) The more that there is held that the mental and physical body is surrounded by, is protected by, that consciousness of the Master that gave, "I will not leave thee comfortless", and the greater the physical can be submerged, the greater will be the activity of the spiritual forces in and through such bodies.

Meditation in Daily Life

Reading 2946-6

But do be consistent; do be persistent and that hour each day as it is used in accordance with the regulations, keeping the body relaxed, use that period as the time for meditation and prayer. Have ye learned (as ye have) the difference between prayer and meditation? Prayer is supplication to God and meditation is listening to His answer.

Reading 1861-12

(Q) *Is it possible to meditate and obtain needed information?*

(A) On any subject! whether you are going digging for fishing worms or playing a concerto!

Reading 2175–6

(Q) *Please suggest best manner of meditation for me.*

(A) As we have indicated to the entity, there must be some ceremony. Choose whatever manner that befits thine own consciousness, whether this is from odors or otherwise. And if odors are chosen, choose sandalwood and cedar to be burned.

In such an atmosphere much of those things that were a part of the experience through those periods of meditation may be brought back.

Then surround the self by thought, as well as by word, with the consciousness of the Christ-Presence. *Then*, and only under such, ye may open the centers for direction.

Reading 1861–18

With the periods set aside for meditation—don't hurry yourself, don't be anxious but closing the self, the conscious mind to anxieties from without—enter within thine own inner temple. There let the voice, the feeling direct; yea, let the spirit of the purpose of self be free in its direction to self.

Attune yourself almost in the same manner as you tune the violin for harmony. For when the body-mind and the soul-mind is attuned to the infinite, there will be brought harmony to the mind and those centers from which impulse arises will aid in the directing of the individual entity to become more sensitive and the material things about the entity may be the better enjoyed. There will not be brought just that we might call satisfaction.

There is much more in anticipation and hope and desire than in being satisfied or gratified. Always know that there is more, if the whole trust is in the Lord.

Reading 803–1

(Q) *How can she best develop her intuitive ability?*

(A) By meditation.

(Q) *And for what purpose should she use it?*

(A) In developing herself and aiding others.

(Q) *Am I in the right work at present?*

(A) This may lead to what will make for the greater development, but in the right work in the present.

Reading 257–87

(Q) *Give body principle to follow for daily meditation as advised, so he will know
how to do it.*

(A) As has been given, when thou prayest enter into thine chamber,
relax the physical body, repeat—not as rote, but as sincerity:

*Let that be my attitude that Thou would have it be! May my thoughts, my acts, be
in accord with the use Thou would have of me!*

This repeat every few seconds for the first fifteen minute period. Then,
if the body loses consciousness—all the better.

(Q) *Reclining or sitting?*

(A) Reclining will be the better, especially in the beginning. Shut out
everything else as far as possible. This will be more and more possible
as this is made in the inner being, to *use me as Thou seest fit, not as I would—
as Thou would have me go!* Then, when there are presented those various
contacts and associations, as was said of old, in the selfsame hour will
there be given thee what should be said or done—but obtain this as
from Him. The body then grows, physically, mentally, spiritually. The
law is sure, the world may pass away—as He has given, "but my word,
my promise, will *not* pass away!"

Reading 620–3

(Q) *What is meant by the experiences I have had concerning [...]?*

(A) These may be better interpreted by self entering into the silence
and answering from those experiences that will be had by this entering
in. First, as is indicated in the affirmations and the lessons of that in
Meditation, ask self consciously and get the answer Yes or No. Ask in
such a manner as Is it this, Is it that? Then enter into the silence with the
inner self and get the answer; ask in such a manner that the spirit of
self, of self's development, answers Yes or No.

Reading 599–1

It would be well if the body would train itself along the subliminal
line.

Go into silence, that is sit for an hour, not so long at first, begin with ten or fifteen minutes, then increase to an hour, sit well up in the chair with both hands on the knees and relieve the mind of everything. Don't think about anything, but leave the mind blank. Let the spiritual come in and take possession of the body. Then he will see and hear from those that he is attuned with. Sometime they will be at different places and different persons. Do not fool with those that are not of a spiritual nature. In this way he will develop himself along this line.

Reading 275–39

(Q) *Outline a method of meditation which will help me the most in my psychic development, giving best time, and prayer.*

(A) As has been indicated, in that manner as seemeth to thine own conscience purge thine body with pure water and with those influences whether in tones of color, of music, or of odors, as the conscience, as the desire of the heart is, so surround self—and with that blessing as He gave, that "May His peace and His blessings surround you as ye enter into that oneness with Him in the inner chamber." And with such a meditation or prayer as: *I Am Thine, O Lord. Use me now as Thou seest fit that I, even in my weakness, may claim thy strength in and through me. Purge me as thou seest I have need of, that I may be the better channel for the manifesting of the love of the Father through the Christ at this time.*

(Q) *What is the best time for meditation for this entity?*

(A) Whenever there is the call, as it were, to prayer, to service, to aid another. Preferably in those hours when there is quiet, either in the evening or the early morning hours.

Reading 412–7

(Q) *What is the meaning of the feeling which I have in meditation?*

(A) More oft it is the fear of "letting go," or at others the interference from without—*from* fear. Yet, as we have given, by the surrounding of self with the Christ, the loving Son's Consciousness, this will be taken away; and the *joy* of knowing ye are a channel of blessing will enter in.

The Physical Body and Meditation

Reading 903–24

(Q) *What is the proper posture for my meditations?*

(A) As has been indicated before, each individual is an entity, each individual has had and *is*—not a law unto itself, but—a development unto *the law!*

That then becomes rather that which is to the entity the more expressive of that being sought to be attained in the experience. Thus as the entity has attained, as the entity has gained in itself, at times the pose or posture would be different. As these vary, meet same.

Remember, how was it given of old? (which may never, never be improved upon!) In the offering of that which would cleanse the body, in the offering of that which would roll away those influences in the experiences of an individual, varied forms and manners were given that they (the forms) might to the *entity* in its inner self find that response of doing and being in accord with the *sources* from which aid, help and understanding is sought.

Hence to each there comes a change. So to this entity. Do not let it become as a rote only, nor as form only; but as chord answering to chord, as the vibrations from each portion of the body to the one purpose in self of being in accord with the divine within, in body, in mind.

Thus it becomes the better.

In some periods it will be found that soft music would aid, though the music may be made by the very activity *of* the concording of the vibrations through the body.

At other periods odors may aid, though these—too—may be as an emanation from the altars of sacrifice within self; or those postures that may bring into play the activity of them all.

(Q) *In her daily life, is she able to discriminate between the divine guidance and that of desire?*

(A) Every one may answer self in this. As He has so oft given, if ye will be silent—even though a moment—ye know. For it is not in the storm, nor in the rage, nor the tempest—but in the still small voice.

Reading 1158–23

(Q) *Will I benefit from lying daily 15 minutes on board with head lower than feet?*

(A) If such a period is used as a period of meditation, very well; but the greater benefit will be obtained from the meditation! Though such a position, of course, will *induce* the flow of influences and forces through the system, by such a deep meditation.

Reading 1861–19

(Q) *What progress has been made toward absorption and elimination of the cataracts?*

(A) These, as we find, are slow, yet sure, if there will be kept, not only the corrections made occasionally, once a month or such—might be the more often but the meditation; and in the meditation, don't meditate *upon,* but listen to the voice within. For prayer is supplication for direction, for understanding. Meditation is listening to the Divine within.

Reading 599–6

Beware of those things as impressed on the mental attitude of body as respecting digestion; for these are things not to be lightly over-ridden; but the general application of self to such conditions are to respond. Then heed, and not be swayed by others to overload system when it should not be; especially with meats and sugars; for there exists—as has been given for the body—much of that as may be applied from within through the application of self to the psychic or mediumistic forces of the body. Well that these be heeded. Be not unmindful of the voices, nor of the visions as come to the inner self. Do not attempt to force such elements; else there is too much of the likelihood of interference from earth forces. Well that the body enter into meditation each evening at a specified time, place, and begin with the 14th chapter of John, and remember these words forward and backward unto the end of the 17th chapter, as has been set out. In *this* association, *this* sphere of communication, may there come none but those that are in accord with the proper and correct development of the inner man; for as this begins, "In my Father's house are many mansions," is spoken of self even as in the end, "Lo, I am with you, even unto the end of the world." Make that presence ever felt within self. No evil may enter. We are through.

Reading 2072–11

(Q) *Please give advice that would help in those times when there is the beginning of Kundalini to rise or there is the circulation of Kundalini through the body. What should be the next step?*

(A) Surround self with that consciousness of the Christ–Spirit; this by the affirmation of "Let self be surrounded with the Christ–Consciousness, and the *directions* be through those activities in the body–force itself."

Do not seek the lower influences, but the Christ–Consciousness.

Reading 275–39

(Q) *Exactly what happens to my physical body during meditation?*

(A) In deep meditation there descends the influences to open the channels along those vistas, as has been given, to the inmost recesses of the Creative Forces in body, that arise then to the varied centers and find expression either through the movements of the body in the hearing of sound, in the consciousness of odors, in the activity of the vision, or there is just the presence that may be read as the open book. Or, to put in other terms, as has been given, the records of time and space—present and future—are upon those films that lie between time and space, and they become attuned to those forces of the Infinite as the cells of the body become attuned to the music of the realms of light and space and time.

Reading 2454–1

(Q) *Do I have sufficient understanding of the spiritual law to bring complete recovery from this apparent illness?*

(A) As has been indicated, without this understanding the body would have collapsed long since! But there are energies lacking. The active forces and principles as indicated are just as divine as mental attitudes, and are at times necessary for *completing* the unison of activity of physical, mental and spiritual being.

(Q) *Why does deep meditation seem to weaken me physically?*

(A) Because there are those centers affected as indicated, through which connections or activity may be said to exist between the spiritual, mental and physical forces. Precautions need to be taken, then, as to overstimulating the activities of the superficial circulation as it coordinates with the mental and spiritual centers. For, deep activity in these directions brings to the body a headache, or a dizziness and a tiredness—which is because of a lack of complete coordination between the superficial and deeper circulation.

Reading 1992-3

(Q) *Is there a meditation that can be used for building the body and keeping it in good condition? Please explain how this might be accomplished?*

(A) Just as the suggestions may be used that have been made to the body through some of the treatments outlined—the *mind* acts upon the resuscitating forces of the physical being, by and through suggestion. Just so there may be the realization that spiritual forces are a part of the whole physical being. For, the *real* being is the spiritual import, intent and purpose, see? Thus a meditation, a centralizing, a localizing of the mind upon those portions of the system affected, or upon the activities needed for the physical being, *influences*, directs the principal forces of the system. And it does resuscitate, if kept in sincerity; not merely said as rote, but that said being put into practical application through the experiences and associations with others—and especially this entity as it works with the developing minds, may see such reactions.

In the meditations, then, *open* the mind, the being, to the influences about same; surrounding self with the consciousness of the healing that is in the Christ-Consciousness, the Christ-awareness.

Thus:

Lord, use Thou me—my body, my mind—in such a way and manner that I, as Thy servant, may fill those lives and hearts and minds I meet—day by day—with such hope and faith and power in Thy might, that it may bring the awareness of Thy presence into the experience of others as well as myself.

Such as these will bring those forces and influences for helpful experiences for the body.

Reading 1861-4

(Q) *How may I bring into activity my pineal and pituitary glands, as well as the Kundalini and other chakras, that I may attain to higher mental and spiritual powers? Are there exercises for this purpose, and if there are, please give them.*

(A) As indicated, first so *fill* the mind with the ideal that it may vibrate throughout the whole of the *mental* being!

Then, close the desires of the fleshly self to conditions about same. *Meditate* upon "*Thy will with me.*" Feel same. Fill *all* the centers of the body, from the lowest to the highest, with that ideal; opening the centers by surrounding self first with that consciousness, "*Not my will but Thine, O Lord, be done in and through me.*"

And then, have that desire, that purpose, not of attaining without *His* direction, but *with* His direction—who is the Maker, the Giver of life and light; as it is indeed in Him that we live and move and have our being.

(Q) *Is there any method whereby I might develop such faculties as a perfect memory; intuition, telepathy, astral projection, and healing of others, as well as myself?*

(A) All healing of every nature comes from the *Divine* within that body, or the body applied to such methods or manners of healing.

The attuning of self—not as to that this or that may be accomplished. But remember, as has ever been given of old, *all* manner of expression, all life, emanates from one source—God! God in thyself; not as "I will, but as Thou wilt."

Let that be the purpose, the import, the intent, the *desire*; and that which is needed for the bringing of its abilities and faculties of every nature in attunement will be done.

And thus give off, in harmonious accent, that as will be pleasing in His sight—the purpose for which each soul enters a material experience.

(Q) *How may I best be used as a channel to be of mental and spiritual assistance to others?*

(A) First by finding self and self's relationship, and the Creative Forces being manifested in thy daily activity, thy daily speech, thy daily conversation, thy daily convocation with thy fellow men; in that each activity is as *unto* the Lord!

Final Thoughts

Reading 1861-18

(Q) *Any method of improving meditation and concentration?*

(A) Just as indicated. This we would keep, but don't be anxious about it. Let it be a necessity to thy better being, rather than giving or having the meditation for better being. It's like whether you are baptized for or baptized to! It's the same application within the inner self. You have the meditation because you desire to be attuned with Creative Forces. You don't have the meditation because it's a duty or because you want to feel better, but to attune self to the infinite! and in attuning self, use your own vocal self; as with the oo–ah–ah—um [AUM]; but do your own vocaling.

(Q) What is the correct way of sounding aum?

(A) That of attuning self by your own vocal cords—not tuning like you are giving vocal orientations.

Reading 281–15

(Q) [560]: How may we avoid becoming rote in meditation and our daily lives?

(A) By visualizing in such manners those meditations that are given out for others, for self; for in aiding others does one aid one's self most. And unless this is so visualized from without self, it becomes rote. But when made, set, or so experienced by the inner self as being an active, living principle within self, it ceases to become rote.

Reading 257–92

(Q) Why do I go to sleep so quickly when I begin the meditation?

(A) Perfect relaxation. There is gradually the taking hold by the inner forces, or inner powers of the body. Train, or set self to retain more and more that which is experienced through such sleep, or such loss of consciousness; for activation is taking place. Remember, the heart doesn't stop beating because you are asleep. The brain doesn't stop acting because you are asleep. Remember all forces; for sleep is as a *sense* of the whole system, and is the great recuperating force. When considered in the same manner, the senses of touch, of seeing, of hearing, of feeling, of all the forces within self, are just as helpful in bringing recuperation, if the diversions are in such a way and manner acted upon to rebuild rather than to destroy all force or strength in the physical body—see? So, in the activating of that sense of sleep, the auditory forces—or those that come through feeling and hearing (which are on guard before the thrones then), then harken to that which is received, even as listening to the program of the best salesman you have sent out! for it *is* the best! for it's before the Throne!

Reading 281-4

(Q) [69]: *Are my meditations bringing results? If not, please help me to accomplish this desire.*

(A) As given, the meditations are bringing results to others, to self. Keep that consciousness that in Him all things are done well. That that is not understood—trust; knowing that there will come the understanding as the awakening to the various laws of love that constitute life in its essence and development through the physical, material, mental and spiritual planes.

Reading 462-8

(Q) *What is my best time for meditation?*

(A) As would be for all, two to three o'clock in the morning is the best time.

(Q) *Any other suitable time?*

(A) *Any* time. For how has the injunction been? "Constant in prayer." This is rather then that the whole attitude be kept in that attitude ever of a thankfulness. And leave it with Him. And go to personal or physical activity in some given direction.

Reading 2982-3

(Q) *What are the best hours for meditation?*

(A) The best hour for meditation is two o'clock in the morning. The better period would be that which will be set as a period in which the body and mind may be dedicated to that. Then keep your promise to self, and to your inner self, and to your Maker, or that to which ye dedicate thy body, mind and soul.

Reading 262-100

(Q) *What is the best time for . . . [meditation for the study group]?*

(A) Either 11 to 12 in the day or 11 to 12 in the evening, or the best time is 2 to 3 in the morning!

Reading 281-6

(Q) *What period of meditation would be best for this body?*

(A) Noon.

Reading 1861-19

(Q) Why is 2 a.m. the best time to meditate?

(A) For the body-mind, as we find, (if it has slept), the activities—of the physical body are as it were, in that vibration where it is between the physical, the mental, and spiritual activities of the body. If it is kept awake, it isn't a good time to meditate, but sleep, and then arise, and purposefully—for in prayer, so in meditation, let it be purposefully, and then don't abuse it—use it. Life is the manifestation of God—of the Creative Forces. So in prayer and in meditation. Prayer—He knoweth what ye have need of, but it is that love, that hope within self, knowing, feeling the desire to approach, thankful, prayerful, and then listen for direction.

Reading 1532-1

(Q) What is the best time for me to meditate?

(A) Early of a morning—six-thirty to seven o'clock.

Reading 1089-8

(Q) What method is best suited for this entity in preparing for periods of meditation?

(A) *Purify* self; as in *any* manner that is in keeping with that as would to the mental self separate self from *worldly* things. Enter in thy inner chamber, thine own conscience, and there pray in secret to the Father that heareth in secret; and He will answer thee openly.

Reading 1158-25

(Q) Please give instructions for conducting a daily deep meditation, with a prayer for use.

(A) The activities of meditation are personal. The preparations for same, to some individuals, are just as necessary as the meditation itself. For, as is comprehended in the minds of most of those who seek to meditate, the attitude of the individual is the greater incentive for such.

Then—we would first have a regular period. Then, in whatever form is most desirable, cleanse the body and mind. Then, relaxing, gently—let this be as the theme, though in thine own words:

"*Lord* of might, of love, be Thou the guide in the things I do and say day by day; that my body, my mind, may fill that purpose Thou hast for me among those of my household, my home, my loved ones, my friends, and all I meet day by day.

"Help me to use each opportunity to be a light bearer for Thee, in His name.

"Keep me, ever."

2

●

Finding Personal Direction Through Meditation and Prayer

Living as a Spiritual Being in the Earth

(Note: Because of their overall counsel and helpfulness, the greatest portions of readings 2528-2, 1472-6, and 657-3 have all been included in this section.)

TEXT OF READING 2528-2

This Psychic Reading given by Edgar Cayce at the office of the Association, Arctic Crescent, Virginia Beach, Va., this 5th day of July, 1942, in accordance with request made by the self—— Mr. [2528], Associate Member of the Ass'n for Research & Enlightenment, Inc.

PRESENT

Edgar Cayce; Gertrude Cayce, Conductor; Gladys Davis, Steno. Mr. [2528] and wife, Mrs. [2794].

READING

Time of Reading 4:10 to 4:40 P. M. Eastern War Time. ..., Va.

GC: You will have before you the body and enquiring mind of [2528], present in this room, who seeks information, advice and guidance as to

how he may be spiritually, mentally and bodily healed. Also you will
consider the invention on which he has been working, with the idea of
saving lives and money, and helping to end the war. You will advise if
he is on the right track to do this with the radar and propeller idea. If so,
whom should he see to make use of it? After giving the information and
guidance needed, you will answer any other questions that may be
asked:

EC: Yes, we have the body, the enquiring mind, [2528], present in this
room.

In considering the physical, mental and spiritual relationships—it
would be necessary that the premises be declared from which any reasoning or application of measures would be taken, that the body may
gain the better concept of the relationships that the mental and the
physical bear with the spiritual forces, in relationship to healing of any
nature.

The body finds itself in a material world of three-dimensional pro-
portions. That which manifests in the mental is from or of a spiritual
nature, but the results in the material or physical manifestation depend
upon the spirit with which the activity is prompted.

This is the law, that was begun when it was first indicated, "God said,
Let there be light, and there was light." This was not as an activity from
the sun, or light as shed from any radial influence, but it was the ability
of consciousness coming into growth from the First Cause.

Then, what is the light? Who is the light?

These are indicated as the sources, the way. For, as has been indicated, without Him there was not anything made that was made. He
came unto His own, and His own received Him not. He was the word
made flesh, yet was rejected of men. This, of course, was because of lack
of understanding, lack of conception as to the purposes or ideals.

Thus an individual, as this entity [2528] finds self in disturbances of a
material nature that are the outgrowth of misunderstanding and mis-
application.

Remember, as has been indicated—and as an individual observes,
when observing individual souls about one—there evidently must have
been, there are, what may be termed confusions even in creation.

These are the results of confusion of instructions or directions by those influences bringing to bear in peoples' lives or activities the result of mental and spiritual activity. These are called accidents or confusions. These may bring into physical expression those hindrances that find expression in both the mental and the material well-being of an individual—as in this experience here with this entity.

In meeting such—these may be met, as indicated, in the light, the way, through those very channels in which those misdirections or misconcepts have occurred.

Healing for the physical body, then, must be first the correct choice of the spiritual import held as the ideal of the individual. For it is returning, of course, to the First Cause, First Principles.

For, there was given to individual souls or entities—as to this entity—the ability to choose, or that light (which is the ability to choose for self)—the *will*; to know self to be one with the whole or the Creative Force, and yet choosing the direction or the spirit, or the purpose, the hope, with which it shall be directed.

These are the premises, then, from and through which the application may be made to self, as for physical, mental and spiritual direction for healing.

There are disturbances in the physical body. This we find, then, as to the body forces, as in this body itself:

Each and every entity, as indicated, finds itself body, mind, soul—or body, mind, spirit. There are, then, those connections, those areas, those activities in a physical body through which spirit and mind function in the physical being for definite reactions or results in the body. These, as we find, are indicated in glands, centers of nerve reactions.

Thus we have a physical being with a circulation through which the assimilation of body forces is taken, distributed through glandular secretion—or mind; that is not conscious mind, but mind of the soul. For, the body *is* the temple of the living God, of light, of life, of hope.

All of these, then, are evidenced in a living human organism.

There are hindrances here.

Those tensions need to be released in the physical forces of the body, in those centers where there are the coordinating forces between the mind and the physical reactions—which are those centers through which the nerve forces in the sympathetic centers coordinate with the cerebrospinal or the central nervous system; or the spirit and mind system with the physical organism—9th dorsal, 4th lumbar, and throughout the cervical areas.

Hydrotherapy and massage will help, not hindering those applications being made, as to aid in coordinating the digestive forces of the activity of the nerves.

But keep away from sedatives!

We would have the hydrotherapy treatments, then; not attempting to make adjustments, but sufficient of heat and water as to relax especially those areas; preferably by a Fume Bath with an equal combination of Witchhazel *and* Camphor.

These would be given about once a week, not more often than that.

As to the mental healing—know first thine own ideal. What is thy ideal? Is the author of thy ideal founded in spirit? Is it the light? Is it the Maker of all that is in the earth, be it perfect or imperfect—according to what man has done with this opportunities? But He in Himself was perfect, and thus becomes the light, the savior, the way, the truth, the life. That is the ideal; not merely in a spiritual sense.

For if that light is that which may control the spirit force in self, and in the choice self may take, does it not also then in the same sense control the results as will be obtained in its materialization in the affairs and the experiences of the individual?

That is the ideal, and the source of all healing. For, as has just been indicated—body, mind, soul or spirit are one, even as Father, Son and Holy Spirit are one. For, they are the materialization of the concept of a three-dimensional individual entity or soul, or consciousness of an entity.

Thus the answer must be in the sources of supply, and in accord with that spirit that maketh a soul, an entity, at-one with the Creative Forces, or the First Cause, or God. *that* makes one whole.

As to the ideals of the entity, and its relationships to the purpose as to save others—these are in the right direction, yes.

The manners in which it may be given to the proper sources may be only through the efforts of the Vice-President, as we find; if there would be worth or the proper coordinated relationships with the ideas and ideals held by the entity.

As to whether this will have its due consideration—it is the same principle as in healing, the same principle as in relationships to individuals and things. Know thy ideal, that idea you express in the formation of those things as would help. Know that self is correct—then leave to Him the part that is the purpose of that to be made, to Him who is life and light; putting it in the proper relationships, yes, just as you would your body in its proper relationship to the mind or spirit of the material conditions.

But do not attempt to do God's work, or hinder same, in His cleansing of a sin-sick world!

Ready for questions.

(Q) *Should any special treatment or attention be given to cramps in legs, aches in shoulders, aches in toe joints, ill feeling in stomach, nausea, dizziness, and nerves?*

(A) These as we find, as indicated, come from the inability of those centers and areas to coórdinate. With even the second or third of such hydrotherapy treatments, we find that all of these conditions should disappear—*if the mind is kept in the proper relationship and balance*, to self and things without! Don't worry! And what is it to worry? Why worry when you can pray? For He is the whole, ye are the part—coordinating thy abilities with the whole.

(Q) *Should anything else be done to give more physical vigor and mental alertness?*

(A) If we attune the physical forces with the best conditions in the mental and spiritual ideals, you'll be plenty alert—if you find the time to be it! But don't overdo self. Don't overtax self. Not that you are to become lazy; be good, but be good for something!

(Q) *Why is it that, although I believe in the power of the Lord, I am unable to get the desired results from my attempts to rely wholly on Him? Wherein have I failed? Is it lack of faith or lack of works, or both?*

(A) Read what has just been indicated here. Do the first things first. Lay the stress on those things that are necessary. Remember, healing—all healing comes from within. Yet there is the healing of the physical, there is the healing of the mental, there is the correct direction from the spirit. Coordinate these and you'll be whole! But to attempt to do a physical healing through the mental conditions is the misdirection of the spirit that prompts same—the same that brings about accidents, the

same that brings about the eventual separation. For it is *law*. But when
the law is coordinated, in spirit, in mind, in body, the entity is capable
of fulfilling the purpose for which it enters a material or physical experience.

Do that.

TEXT OF READING 1472-6

This Psychic Reading given by Edgar Cayce at his home on
Arctic Crescent, Virginia Beach, Va., this 19th day of June,
1938, in accordance with request made by self——Mrs.
[1472], Active Member of the Association for Research &
Enlightenment, Inc.

PRESENT

Edgar Cayce; Gertrude Cayce, Conductor; Gladys Davis,
Steno. Hugh Lynn Cayce.

READING

Time of Reading Set bet. 10:30 to 11:30 A. M. Taken 12:40 to
1:30 P. M. Eastern Standard Time. N.Y.C.

GC: You will have before you the entity [1472] born May 5, 1880 in
Bowling Green, Va., and who is in her apartment at the ..., New York City.
This entity seeks enlightenment and help in her work, in her human
relationships and problems which are presented. She seeks release from
her present duties for the utilization of her gifts and talents along lines
more in accord with her training and abilities. In answering the questions which she has submitted, give both the retarding and developing
factors in her relationships that the entity may serve more and find the
greatest possible development in this experience.

EC: Yes, we have the records of the entity here, now called [1472];
with the information that has been given respecting same.

In the study or the analysis of the conditions and circumstances that
are a portion of the entity's experience, if these are still considered problems, detriments, because here or there there is a latent or manifested
aversion, then these will—with the under standing, as the entity should

have—still remain problems; and little there may be done to release self so long as there is the recognition of problems, of animosities, of likes or dislikes as related to the purposes

This has been a portion of the entity's training, and yet the entity seeks for the use of that in which it has been trained?

How readest thou those conditions that were a part of thy development through those periods in which the entity as the teacher, as the prophetess, sought to prepare its peoples, those with whom it came in contact, for those lessons that were and are a part of the experience of each and every soul that enters the material sojourn for a purposeful life?

Have ye learned that as He gave, and as ye proclaimed as the manner and way in which paths would be made straight? that if thine enemy smite thee, turn the other cheek? and he that looketh on a body to lust has already done those things that are not in keeping with true, pure lives? or if ye listen to those who would tempt thee for this or that purpose wherein it might make thy activities of ease and comfort without the thought of that it would bring into the experiences of others?

What meaneth these? As He gave—love alone begetteth love; purity alone begetteth purity. These things then should be cultivated in thy experience, and in thy dealings with thy fellow man.

Do ye have one standard for he whom thou likest and to whom ye are drawn, and another standard for they that would despitefully use you? Do ye have one measurement for those who would praise, and another for those who would counsel or rebuke thee?

Have ye forgotten that whom the Lord loveth He chasteneth, He purgeth? even as His own, in those experiences through which He was led, in those associations and relations with those He loved as His companions, as His neighbors?

These are all a part of thy own experience, and in thy dealings with thy fellow man these must become not only tenets, not only for the use and application in the experiences of others but they must enter into, they must be a part of thy own dealings with problems (as ye call them), situations (if ye like), stumbling-stones (if ye set them up as such).

Rather let them be that upon which ye will rise as upon the wings of thought, that make for that building into the experiences as to bring those awakenings, those awarenesses of Him whom ye proclaimed so thoroughly, into the hearts and minds.

For as Mind is the Builder, that ye dwell upon, that ye cultivate, *that* is the manner of fruit ye bear in thy daily life.

For the fruits of the spirit—yea, that as is sought; and to be loved in thy own life—are peace, harmony; not at the expense of thy Lord, but with Him keep the paths straight! "For if ye love me, I and the Father will come and abide with thee."

These are not mere words. They may be thy own experience, they may be thy very life!

Seek not for the fame or the fortune that alone makes for those things that hinder and belittle humbleness and service. For he that is the greatest is indeed the servant of all. He that would have life must indeed give life, if he would know that life is indeed the expression of that we worship as the Father–God.

TEXT OF READING 657-3

This psychic reading given by Edgar Cayce at the David E. Kahn home, 44 West 77th St., Apt. 14-W, New York City, this 24th day of November, 1934, in accordance with request made by the self——[657], Active Member of the Ass'n for Research & Enlightenment, Inc.

PRESENT

Edgar Cayce; Hugh Lynn Cayce, Conductor; Gladys Davis, Steno. [657] and friend.

READING

Time of Reading 1:25 to 2:05 P. M. Eastern Standard Time. New York City.

(Entity. Mental & spiritual reading with special reference to his affairs that will make possible a greater development in this present plane. Questions.)

EC: Yes, we have the entity here, [657], and those conditions mental, material and spiritual that surround the body physical.

In giving that which may be helpful to the entity, much that has been given might be repeated as respecting the manner of approach this entity—as others—should make to the experiences in which a manifested soul finds itself in this present sojourn:

Each soul enters an experience for that purpose of an expression of that gained either in the ascendancy or in lessons to be learned that there may be with the soul itself that experience such as to make the soul one with, and an expression of, that Creative Force which manifests itself in a material experience.

Oft do there come confusions to an entity, a soul, through the entanglements of self-expression rather than that entity, that soul, being a channel for the manifestation and the expression of that such a soul has gained in its experiences in material or in matter.

Hence when these confusions arise, there may be an entering into the holy of holies within the self, where the promise has been ever that there thy Lord may meet thee and be that guide, that guard to that inner self for the greater blessings not only for self but that of which the entity, the soul, is the expression—and gives forth in its contact daily a manifestation of that it, the soul, feels, desires, makes as the expression of that it, that entity, that soul, has gained.

It is not as to how much knowledge one has that counts, nor as to how much understanding even; though if there is had the correct understanding it, the entity, knows, feels, gives that expression of same. And it is what the entity does *about* that it knows that counts, not what it knows. For the entity–soul's growth is ever from within. It is not as to what others may think, as to what others may do. But let thy desire, thy will, ever be: "Others may do as they may, but for me and my house, my body (of clay) we will serve the living God."

This entity, [657], has entered in the present experience for a definite purpose, for the clarifying and the purifying and the consecrating of a definite portion of its abilities, its qualities, its activities, for a growth. There has been in the experience of the entity the necessity of the pruning of much of the own ego, that the I *am* may find the greater expression. Yet there has ever been the promise into the hearts and souls of those that seek to know, that to those who knock it may be opened; that ye may know that the acceptable year of the Lord, is at hand, that ye may make thy paths straight in *His* way. Then, let thy prayer be, "Not my way, Lord. Have Thine own way with me, that I may ever in this experience—of every nature, of every kind—be as a channel of blessings to those I contact day by day, in every way, in every manner; and as the call comes may I answer, *'Here am I, use me, send me where Thou seest—as Thou seest—is best that my soul, my mind—yea, my body—may be a living example, known and read of men always!'"*

Ready for questions.

(Q) *Would you advise that I change my profession?*

(A) As we find, and as has been indicated in the experiences of the entity, the profession as chosen offers a channel through which the entity, the body, may be a greater service to the fellow man. Other channels may offer greener pastures in the material things, yea—but how lacking are the laborers in the vineyard wherein not only the bodies of thy fellow man may be aided but through such channels, through such measures, lessons may be learned, and the life and the experience be filled with the opportunities that are for those who have consecrated themselves for such! Remember Him that gave, heal ye the bodies—yea, fear him who may destroy both the body and the soul! For in these channels do we find the greater service may be rendered. Then, choose thou *this* day whom ye will serve. For there is set before thee life and death, good and evil. How readest thou? How choosest thou? For, as given, ye that serve the fellow man—ye that would serve thy fellow man—lend unto the Lord, and *He* will repay.

(Q) *What can I do personally to help improve my financial condition?*

(A) That these conditions have in the past offered, and do in the present offer great obstacles from the human or the material standpoint is obvious. But he that considereth the body and the attributes of same first, chooseth unwisely. That these must be met for the peace of the mind is a portion of that which must be met in that holy of holies, and *there*—and there alone should the entity, the body, the mind, find the answer. There is in the very make-up of the body-mind the speculative instinct, or fact. Facts in the material must be met by material situations. Facts in the mental must be met by the mental and the reason. And those that seek for spiritual life in material things are following after folly. But those that seek in the spiritual the mental *and* the material expressions of self and associations, are wise! Hence, then, use that thou hast in hand. Be guided to put the proper evaluations, the proper stress where it—the stress—is due; and ye will find that thou wilt be guided in doing those things that are for the best. There are to come, and are eminent in the experience of the entity in speculative channels, those periods when those that seek such shall be the material gainers; and these are in those specific fields of activities in the utilities of this and of other great nations. And by the indulgence in same there may come those material gains. But they that live by such shall die by such. For they that live by the sword must abide by the sword's decision. They that live by the spirit shall be alive indeed! And yet these are a portion of the entity's experience. How, first, will ye use that which has and that may come from the use of the material gains? How hast thou used them in the past? Art thou worthy in thine own meeting with thy Lord in His holy place to claim that thou may be entrusted with ten talents when thou hast used two badly? Hast thou the claim that thou may be given fifty talents when ten have been mislaid?

When ye have found grace and favor in Him that is the Father of mercy and peace and harmony and understanding, *then* these will be given thee in these fields. Calumet, to be sure, is ripe for many decisive changes that may come both ways, but as to how—Let the Lord thy God tell thee; not of silver, not of gold, but the God that stands with thee as thou standest for thy brother in the day of need, and when and as thou showest mercy so will it be shown thee!

(Q) *Do you find that it would be advisable for me to share professional offices with another doctor?*

(A) Provided these are, of course, in such accord that their purposes, their aims, their desires, their policies—yea, even in more material their tactics—are compatible.

(Q) *Whom would you advise?*

(A) Any of those associations where these are to be had. For, as is the experience of the entity from all of its approaches to the true spiritual natures of things, as ye seek, as ye send out in and through thine inner self those needs, *who*—who is the provider? Though man in his strength and in his wisdom may work, labor, toil, who giveth increase? Who pointeth the way? Who bringeth it to pass in thine experience? Art

thou, wilt thou keep in that way? Then these may be brought about—
the correct ones, the correct understandings.

(Q) *Would you advise that I seek to make such a change, and when?*

(A) By the first of the year.

(Q) *Should I change my professional location of offices?*

(A) Of course, these may be answered in the same way and manner—
as one seeks truly within the self. This is only bantering questions, when
we consider what has just been given thee as the basis of truth wherein
a life, an experience, a soul, an entity, may find the answer to any question that may arise within its own experience. How, ye may ask, is the
step by step in which I may find such an answer? First, in thine meditation ask the material mind, is it yes or no—and thou wilt receive the
answer; as a vision, as a word. Then take it to thine inner self and let the
answer be given thee then from within. And thou wilt *know*, and thou
wilt it be made aware within every fibre of thine body. For, as ye well
know, my son, in thine inner self, each atom of thy body *must* coordinate, *cooperate*, one with another, that ye in thine physical begin may
have health, or even balance that thy mind, thy entity—yea, thy soul-
body—may have the better channel in which to serve. For indeed thine
body is the temple of the living God. If thou hast desecrated it, or dost
discrete it, what is the answer?

Finding Direction and Purpose in Daily Life
Reading 5368-1

For this entity we would find, then, that spiritual counsel that is latent and manifested must be made more manifest in the activities of the
entity, if there would be those accomplishments which may be had
materially, mentally, spiritually.

True, we would magnify the virtues, and these are many; we would
minimize the faults, and this should be the policy of the entity.

The chosen field of service or activity in the present is very good but
these activities are not all that the body may accomplish, for in the
analyzing of itself, it is not that the ego is to be so manifested as to think
more highly of itself than it should, yet know deep within the heart and
soul that ye are a child of the living God. The earth and the fullness,
though, is His and with thy trust wholly in Him as thy guide, through

prayerful meditations as to choices to be taken here, and not just hunches but rather as with the voice within, there is little that this entity may not accomplish . . .

Astrologically we find that Mercury, Mars, Jupiter, Venus are all parts of the consciousness of the soul–entity. Thus no one will ever call this entity lazy. Sure it gets tired, sure it needs recreation, but not the character of recreation that it sometimes is thought or felt, but rather know change of activity as may be indicated in Mars and not getting angry about anything but keeping in the Jupiterian influence of activities, of things, knowing that these work together for good to those who love the Lord. This doesn't mean just being "goody-goody", but good for something—something definite. Be the best husband there is on the road, be the best salesman in the whole group and you will find that in a very short while there will be much difference, if those set periods are adhered to—not just something to take up a little time, but set a definite period morning or evening, or both even, though it be five or ten minutes—let nothing interfere, pray. Then live like you pray. Then listen, and ye may be very sure the answer will come back to you and ye will soon find everyone much gladder to see you coming. Ye will find all will be ready to assist you in being the best of whatever ye choose as the active service, and soon ye will be given a new place in the general organization where ye can carry on to greater expansion in preparation, in expanding the fields of service with those with whom ye are associated . . .

And when ye pray, give thanks daily, for that ye are given in hand by Him, who is the giver of all good and perfect gifts.

Reading 3624–1

First, here, begin with the mental attitude. For here there must be more purposefulness, more general planning in the hopes and desires of the mental and physical body. The spirit is willing, the flesh has proven weak.

We would begin first, with the formulating of policies and attitudes for the balancing of the life principles and purposes. It is just as necessary that there be food for the spiritual and mental man as for the physical man—and this applies to self.

Take time first to be holy. Don't let a day go by without meditation and prayer for some definite purpose, and not for self, but that self may be the channel of help to someone else. For in helping others is the greater way to help self.

Do take plenty of time for rest. Do take time for plenty of definite labors. Working with the husband is very good, but here you often get cross and are in a manner closed from some associations and activities. But take time to work, to think, to make contacts for a social life and for recreation. This old adage might well apply: After breakfast, work a while, after lunch rest a while, after dinner walk a mile. This as a recreation may be a helpful, balanced experience for this life. As these purposes are set in motion, let it not be "Well, I'll do this sometime" but set all of these in motion for at least a week.

Reading 3976-21

Let thy life, thy experience then, be not without purpose.

What do ye then purpose to do with His promises to thee?

In *this* land ye may give praise for freedom of speech, for the opportunities to raise thy voice in *whatever* way and manner ye choose.

For know, as He taught, the principles of life are that as ye do unto the least of thy brethren ye do unto thy Maker.

Then, as ye give thanks, as ye give praise to thy friends for kindnesses, for gentlenesses, for those things that make thy experience more bearable in a cruel world—under circumstances oft where a troubled heart is made lighter—how much greater in this day, then, that is set aside by thy laws, by the judgments of thy governors and of thy president—how much *more* ye would give thanks to God!

For it is in Him indeed that ye live, that ye move and have thy being. Let thy heart then be glad.

And as has been indicated, let each raise his voice in thanksgiving for *all* that has, that may come to pass in the experience of each *soul* that prays, *"Thy will, O God, be done in me—now. Not as I will, but as Thou would have me go."*

Pray that peace may be in the minds and hearts of those who direct the destiny of the many, throughout the world. For they are *not* in power of *themselves*, but that *ye*—too—may learn a lesson to *do*, and to seek to do, the will of thy Father; and not to do that which is *in* direct contradiction to that of praise to thy Lord, thy God.

Keep then that Day in praise, in thanksgiving, in such ways, such a manner that ye show to thy conscience that what ye worship as thy God is aware of *thy* appreciation of *life!*

Reading 2995-1

Do not think in self as to how ye may take advantage of someone else, or how ye may attain fame or glory. For these are thine own already. For if God be with thee, who can be against thee?

Art thou with Him? This ye ask and may ask and find within self. For, as He has given, "If ye call I will hear." And He has promised to meet thee within thine inner self.

Then in prayer, in meditation, in longing, in hoping—but in doing the things and being the things in thine inner self ye hope for and long for—these are the manners and the ways of approach, and of overcoming those tendencies which arise in the emotions.

Not as one to be long-faced. For, the earth is the Lord's and the fullness thereof—in *joy!* Do not see the dark side too oft. Turn it over—there's another side to every question. Cultivate in self humor, wit. Ye enjoy it in others, others enjoy it in thee. But too oft it becomes to thee foolishness. *Know* that thy Lord, thy God, *laughed*—even at the Cross. For He wept with those who wept, and rejoiced with those who rejoiced.

Reading 257-250

(Q) *Please advise me how to aid myself to fulfill my affirmation, "O God, please let my inclination be that, that thou would have it be. Let my thoughts and acts be in accordance with that, that thou would have me be."*

(A) These are well. So long as these affirmations, this meditation and prayer, are not mere words to justify self, there needs be little doubt. For He, the Father-God, is not short in meting out His grace and mercy. For, as has been given of old, "The mercy of the Lord endureth forever, to those that seek to do His biddings."

Then, study to show thyself approved. Let this be in thy mind as ye approach each proposition, each condition that deals with *all* problems. For, while these appear oft to be very far apart, or even foreign one to another, ye know that thy meditation is that principle, that purpose upon which this government was brought into being.

Then with such an idea, such an ideal, in thy dealings with the problems of war, of preparedness, of all phases of moral, economic, and conditions to come, ye will be the closer in keeping with that needed.

Each day, then, just give thanks. Keep humble in the blessings He bestows upon thee, and in the favor that He grants thee in the sight of those who have been and are privileged to be the channels through which all forms of preparation are made for carrying on, waging a war against oppression, against slavery, against the disregard of such principles.

Do not become egotistical, officious, or other than as David of old gave, letting it be said of thee in thine own conscience: I seek thy face, O Lord—thy counsel, thy precepts—as I deal with my fellow man in carrying forward those principles in this period of disturbance among nations . . .

Reading 1286–1

Yet the greater blessings that the entity in its activity rendered the people in that experience were in the building of individual homes.

And this will become a part of the entity's experience in this sojourn. For within the next two and a half to three years there should come into the experience that association, the relations with one who was as a helpmeet to the entity during that sojourn.

For, as has been indicated from the innate experience as well as from the longings within, a home—*home*—with all its deeper, inner meanings, is a portion of the entity's desire; to know, to experience, to have the "feel" of, to have the surroundings of that implied by the word *home!* Is it any wonder then that in all of thy meditation, Ohm—O-h-m-mmmmm has ever been, is ever a portion of that which raises self to the highest influence and the highest vibrations throughout its whole being that may be experienced by the entity?

Thus does it behoove the entity to find in those activities that which will bring about in the experience that which will make home—*home*—as a *reality;* close to nature. Not in the strife and turmoil, not in cities, not where there are the surroundings of those forces that bespeak of the commercial life, but that as of *nature!* That as was given by the entity then as the priestess of those peoples, that made for the dedicating of their lives, that which would bring into the experience of each soul its relationships to *nature* as it manifests itself in its defiance of, in its laws with, in its beauties of, in its troubles with humankind; as it meets same in the rain, the sun, the storm, the dew, the beauty of the sun and the moon and all the glories of nature itself become rather as the song of the entity in its experience; when the sons of God with the voices of the winds sang together of the heralding of the glory of the noonday to the sons of God! That became as the chant of the entity in that experience, in the name Tulu.

In the application of same, much might be said in these directions. For these become so much a portion of the entity; and in those closer relationships with nature, with heaven, with the earth, with all the toils and troubles of same, with all the activities that come with same may be found the greater peace and harmony.

For what becometh to this soul that seeks so beautiful and joyous as the music in the rain or in the babbling brook or in the moonlight or in the noonday sun or in the beauty of the rose or the smile of the child! These become as those that give to the entity the greater expressions of the love of a merciful heavenly Father. For they bespeak of the promise of the rest of a home, of an ohm [?] with Him.

Reading 2791-1

(Q) *Please give further guidance for stabilizing my emotional life and directions for new interest and activities for mental and spiritual development.*

(A) Study well that which has been indicated here. Much of this may open to thee an entirely new field of thought, of activity. But first learn that as ye serve others, ye serve thy Lord, thy God. And remember this—not as a goody-goody, not as one who would shut self away, but—it is rather one that goes about doing good.

Do that.

Let this be thy prayer, then, oft:

Lord, Thou art God! In Thy hands I give my life. Make me that Thou would have me be, through the promises that are set in the Christ, the Lord.

Discerning One's Next Step in Life

Reading 1246-4

In seeking the answer then to any problem, the entity may find same if it will first—the mental self—make definite efforts to gain the answer through its own mental reasoning; analyzing the whole situations much in the same manner as there is a visualizing even before there is a drawing of how an individual room or suite or several would look under the varying treatments with the varying characters of lights or the like, as well as woods and shapes and forms and the like.

If the whole situations are taken into consideration, there must necessarily be first the analysis of the character as it were of the individual for whom such might be prepared.

So, in the analyzing of the problems for self, analyze same much in the same manner; taking into consideration the individuals, their characters, their associations, their background, their outlook upon their relationships with others. And have the answer, Yes or No.

Then take the same considerations, with the answer, into the deep meditation and let there still be the answer from the deeper within—but abide by that given thee! Do not become one that asks and does not abide by the answers! For they would soon become as naught to thee!

For the promises are that He will meet thee within; that He is thy life, thy meat, thy *daily* understanding!

Then use that thou hast in hand. Not to thine own glory but that there may be, through thy *giving* of thyself as a channel, a blessing to others, in every phase of their experience, in *His* name!

Reading 270-33

(Q) *Please guide me with information that will enable me to become of greater service to my fellow man.*

(A) There's none better than we have given, and as may be followed by that which may be brought to the awareness of self through the *practical* application of those meditative forces that come by setting aside a definite time, a period during each day's activity when there will be the purifying of the body, as in accord with that which would make for consecrating of self in all of its efforts, all of its abilities, and entering into the holy of holies within self for that talk with thy God within thyself. These efforts on the part of any soul will bring those things that make for the greater peace and happiness and the abilities to meet those emergencies of every nature that arise within the physical and mental bodies of a living body. For then the God–forces that are the creative energies of the soul–mind will become the ruling forces in the life and in its activity in same; making for those abilities wherein any soul, any entity, may become the greater service, the greater factor in its associations with its fellow man. It is not how much one knows that counts, but how well one applies that it knows; in just being, doing, thinking, that which is pointed out to self through such constant, consistent, *practical* dependence upon the Creative Forces that have promised ever to meet one—every one—when sought. And there will come that which is for the greater development in the soul forces of such an one that seeks.

Reading 666-1

In a *development* of mental concentration, the better will *always* be found to be made by entering into the silence; not as is to the body that of merely *rote* to go through a performance, but as an accomplishment of the mental and physical body to create within the physical and mental *being* of the body *that* ability to *control* or *direct* its activities in whatever *chosen* manner or way it would direct same! In entering into the silence, do so in a prayerful manner, *knowing* in what is set to self *as* an *ideal;* not an idea, but let the *ideas* emanate *from* that accomplished in entering into the silence, or two to five minutes each day communing with that of the Creative Forces as may manifest themselves in a mental, a material, and a spiritual way and manner.

Reading 3250-1

(Q) *What will help me most in coming to right decisions as to my life?*
(A) Prayer and meditation, to be sure. For, as He has given, "Behold I stand at the door and knock. If ye will open I will enter in."

Then, in thine own mind, decide as to whether this or that direction is right. Then pray on it, and leave it alone. Then suddenly ye will have the answer, yes or no.

Then, with that Yes or No, take it again to Him in prayer, "Show me the way." And yes or No will again direct thee from deep within.

That is practical direction.

As has been pointed out, experiences, visions, mean much to thee. For thou hast seen the outpouring of the Holy Spirit. It may not be withheld from thee now, if ye seek same.

Reading 1242-6

(Q) *Any other advice for this body, either physical or spiritual?*

(A) There should be kept, to be sure, a hopeful, constructive attitude as to its material and physical welfare, as well as in its spiritual application and spiritual attitudes. For each soul should gain that understanding that whatever may be the experience, if there is not resentment, if there is not contention, if there is not the giving of offense, it is for then that soul's own understanding, and will build within the consciousness of the soul itself that which may bring the greater understanding of the spiritual in the physical body.

Then let the prayer, the meditation, ever be:

"Here am I, Lord. Thou knowest my faults, Thou knowest my weaknesses: Yet I am Thine, and Thou would use me as Thou seest fit. Let Thy will, O God, be done in and through me, in such measures that I may be a channel of blessings to others. For as I forgive, may I be forgiven. As I bless may I be blessed by Thy love and Thy presence.

"Then keep me in the ways, in body, in mind, in spirit, that I should go."

Reading 3654-1

(Q) *How can I extend the borders or my consciousness to achieve greater spiritual development and illumination?*

(A) Open thy heart, thy mind to the prayer indicated: *Here am I, emptied of all my own desire; selfless before Thee, O God. Fill Thou my heart and soul with the purpose to be a channel of blessing to someone today.*

Reading 1472-12

Then, in this era, this age of changes being wrought, it behooves the entity (as everyone), in its relationships in any manner, to impress upon others in every walk of life—not impelling by force, but by love—to *try* God; to listen to the voice within; to open self to the love that is manifested in gentleness and kindness, and not to the lust for power nor to what others may say, but rather keeping in that attitude which He expressed in that period of manifestation when He said, "Others may do as they may, but as for me, I will serve a *living* God," not one far off. Not one who may not be touched by the infirmities of those who are oppressed and cry unto Him; but when ye pray, when ye cry, that prayer, that cry, must be consistent with the life that is lived in relationship to others day by day.

Indeed man through all periods has with one voice blessed God and with the same cursed his brother. This, as the entity understands, should not be! Yet it is such in the world today that is bringing the seeking for might and power.

As to the manners in which the entity applies those influences which it attained or gained through the periods when it again announced to the children of men the great and mighty day of the Lord being at hand—ye are coming to the realization that the fulfilling of that promise in Him is *today*; for He *is* the way, the truth and the light!

It is no longer, then, afar off; but lo, it is within the heart and mind of each soul—*everywhere!*

For, whosoever *will* may take of the cup of life, and drink—in such measures that the thirsting is no more for those things that put fear and dread into the hearts of the children of men.

For it is neither in this temple, that city, nor the other land, but in thine own heart, in thine own mind.

And *this* ye are to proclaim in thy service through the activities in which ye may be engaged, of whatever nature; whether as the assistant in the script for thine own broadcasts, or in that help ye may give to others.

Know, even as He hath given, if ye enter into the closet of thine own consciousness and *there* give that prayer, that longing, *He* will reward thee openly—as He does thy brethren.

Personal Prayers and Affirmations
Reading 357-9

Well that the body keep that constructive attitude of relying upon creative forces within self, as related to the spiritual and mental attitudes of the body (this is referring to mental forces, to be sure). These thoughts as a meditation, as we find would be well:

Into Thy keeping, Heavenly Merciful Spirit, I commit myself: in body, in mind, in spirit. Help Thou me in my choice of activities of every nature as to become more and more a living channel of blessings to others: that I may be a light in Jesus, the Christ, to others.

Reading 2619-1

In the mental and spiritual attitude, let the prayer of the body be—not merely in words but in the deeper feeling, put into thy own words:

"Father, God! in Thy love, in Thy mercy, remember Thou thy servant, as she seeks to know Thy face and Thy way with me. Use Thou, O God, my power of discernment, my abilities in the earth, in Thy service. Be Thou, O God, the strength, the help, just now."

Reading 709-1

(Q) How can I bring about a more agreeable attitude toward housekeeping and homemaking?

(A) This, as indicated, is a portion of the mental and spiritual influences within self. Let this thy prayer and meditation be, morning, noon and night:

Let there be done in and through my body, O Lord, that Thou seest will fit same for the better, the greater, the more direct manifestation of Thy self to my fellowman. May I be a channel of blessings to someone in the name of Him that promised to be—and to give—that we would ask in His name!

Reading 849-76

(Q) Please give a prayer for meditation to be used while writing the pamphlets, the book, and the poem?

(A) *Father-Mother-God! in Thy mercy, in Thy love, be Thou the guide just now, as I seek in humility and in earnestness to present that which may give my fellow man a better and a more perfect insight into the love which was manifested by Jesus, my Lord and my God. Help, Thou, O God, my every effort.*

Reading 282-6

(Q) Give prayers and affirmations specially adapted to the body-mind in his present condition.

(A) Father, may there be in me that mind, that desire, which prompted the living of the life of Thy Son in this material world.

May I be drawn nearer and nearer to that understanding of the purposes of the manifestations of life, making my will one with Thy will, feeling and realizing Thy presence abiding day by day in my every experience; realizing life's activities are the manifestations of Thy love.

Keep me in the right way. Amen.

Reading 1530–1

(Q) Am I strong enough, spiritually and otherwise, to take it on at this time?

(A) Putting thy trust in Him, counseling oft with Him within thine inner self, yes. Without Him and that strength which comes from the closer walks and associations with Him, no.

Let that purpose ever be, in all thine heart, in all thy meditations:

"Have Thy way, O Lord, with me! Let me day by day, in every way, be the greater channel of blessings to those i meet day by day.

"Let my love for my fellow man so fill my desires and my hopes that I see not faults—not as a condoning but as they each fulfilling that purpose Thou would have with them!

"For I know that Thou hast not willed that any soul should perish, but that with every temptation, every trial, Thou hast prepared a way that will eventually bring that soul to the consciousness of Thy abiding presence.

"And let me so live, so act, that that consciousness may ever be mine."

3

•

Spiritual Development, Purposes, and Ideals

The Importance of Having a Spiritual Purpose in Life

(Note: Because of the way in which readings 987-4 and 274-3 specifically address the overall topic of this chapter, both readings have been included in their entirety.)

TEXT OF READING 987-4 F 49

This Psychic Reading given by Edgar Cayce at his home on Arctic Crescent, Virginia Beach, Va., this 2nd day of November, 1937, in accordance with request made by the self—Mrs. [987], Associate Member of the Ass'n for Research & Enlightenment, Inc.

PRESENT

Edgar Cayce; Gertrude Cayce, Conductor; Gladys Davis, Steno. Mrs. [987].

READING

Time of Reading 4:00 to 4:45 P. M. Eastern Standard Time. New York City.

GC: You will have before you the entity, [987], present in this room, who seeks a Mental and Spiritual Reading, with information, advice and guidance as to her development and proper expression in the earth. You will answer the questions she submits, as I ask them:

EC: Yes, we have the entity, [987].

In giving the analysis of the mental and spiritual self, many are the conditions that arise as questions in the experience of the entity. These to be sure must be approached as to the purpose and the desires of the *spiritual* self.

That there may be a more perfect understanding, much as to those that have been the experiences of the entity as a soul–entity must be referred to.

For, life—or the motivative force of a soul—is eternal; and that portion of same that is motivated by the mental and spiritual attributes of an entity has experienced, does experience the influences that have guided or prompted same through its sojourns.

For each soul seeks expression. And as it moves through the mental associations and attributes in the surrounding environs, it gives out that which becomes either for selfish reactions of the own ego—to express—or for the *I am* to be at–one with the Great *I Am that I Am.*

What then are the purposes for the activities of an entity in a material plane, surrounded with those environs that make for self–expressions or self–activities in the various ways and manners?

What meaneth these? That self is growing to that which it, the entity, the soul, is to present, as it were, to the Great *I am* in those experiences when it is absent from materiality.

These become hard at times for the individual to visualize; that the mental and soul may manifest without a physical vehicle. Yet in the deeper meditations, in those experiences when those influences may arise when the spirit of the Creative Force, the universality of soul, of mind—not as material, not as judgments, not *in* time and space but *of* time and space—may become lost in the Whole, instead of the entity being lost in the maze of confusing influences—then the soul visions arise in the meditations.

And the centers becoming attuned to the vibrations of the bodily force, these give a vision of that as may be to the entity an outlet for the self–expressions, in the beauties and the harmonies and the activities that become, in their last analysis; just being patient, longsuffering, gentle, kind. *These* are the fruits of the spirit of truth; just as hates, malice and the like become in their growths those destructive forces in creating, in making for those things that are as but tares, confusions, dissensions in the experiences of an entity.

Those then are the purposes of the entrance of an entity into a material plane; to choose that which is its ideal.

Then ask thyself the question—gain the answer first in thy physical consciousness:

"What is my ideal of a *spiritual* life?"

Then when the answer has come—for it has been given by Him that is Life, that the kingdom of God, the kingdom of heaven, is within; and we view the kingdom of God without by the application of those things that are of the spirit of truth—These then answered, ye seek again in the inner consciousness:

"Am I true to my ideal?"

These become then the answers. This and that and the other; never as pro and con. For the growth in the spirit is as He has given; ye *grow* in grace, in knowledge, in understanding.

How? As ye would have mercy shown thee, ye show mercy to those that even despitefully use thee. If ye would be forgiven for that which is contrary to thy own purposes—yet through the vicissitudes of the experiences about thee, anger and wrath give place to better judgment—ye, too, will forgive those that have despitefully used thee; ye will hold no malice. For ye would that thy Ideal, that Way ye seek, hold no malice—yea, no judgment—against thee. For it is the true law of recompense; yea, the true law of sacrifice.

For not in sacrifice alone has He sought His judgments, but rather in mercy, in grace, in fortitude; yea, in divine love.

The shadows of these are seen in thy inner experience with thy fellow man day by day. For ye have seen a smile, yea a kind word, turn away wrath. Ye have seen a gentleness give hope to those that have lost their hold on purpose, other than the satisfying of an appetite—yea, other than satisfying the desires of the carnal mind.

Hence as ye give, ye receive. For this is mercy, this is grace. This is the beauty of the inner life lived.

Know then it is not that judgment is passed here or there. For know that God looketh upon the heart and He judgeth rather the purposes, the desires, the intents.

For what seekest thou to lord (laud) in thy life? Self intent? Know ye not that it was selfishness that separated the souls from the spirit of life and light? Then only in the divine love do ye have the opportunity to become to thy fellow man a saving grace, a mercy, yea even a savior.

For until ye have in thy own material associations known thyself to be the saving grace to someone, ye may not know even the whole mercy of the Father with the children of men.

Then it is not of rote; it is not ritual that has made for those influences in thine own experience; but in whom, in what hast thou put thy trust?

He has promised to meet thee within the temple of thine own body. For as has been given, thy body is the temple of the living God; a tabernacle, yea, for thy soul. And in the holy of holies within thine own consciousness He may walk and talk with thee.

How? How?

Is it the bringing of sacrifice? Is it the burning of incense? Is it the making of thyself of no estate?

Rather is it that ye *purpose!* For the try, the purpose of thine inner self, to HIM is the righteousness. For He hath known all the vicissitudes of the earthly experience. He hath walked through the valley of the shadow of death. He hath seen the temptations of man from every phase that may come into thine own experience; and, yea, He hath given thee, "If ye will love me, believing I am able, I will deliver thee from that which so easily besets thee at *any* experience."

And it is thus that He stands; not as a Lord but as thy Brother, as thy Savior; that ye may know indeed the truth that gentleness, kindness, patience, brotherly love, beget—in thy heart of hearts, with Him—that peace, that harmony. Not as the world knoweth peace but as He gave: "That peace I give you; that ye may know that thy spirit, yea thy soul, beareth witness with me that ye are mine—I am thine," even as the Father, the Son, the Holy Spirit.

Even so may thy soul, thy mind, thy body, become aware of that which renews the hope, the faith, the patience within thee.

And until ye show forth in His love that patience, ye cannot become aware of thy relationship with Him. Even as He has given, in patience ye become aware of being that soul—that seeketh the Father's house that is within even thine own consciousness.

How? How, then, may ye approach the throne?

Turn thou within. As ye meditate, give forth in thine *own* words these thoughts:

"Father, God, Maker of Heaven and Earth! I am Thine—Thou art mine! As I claim that kinship with that Holy love, keep Thou me in that consciousness of Thy presence abiding with me: that I may be that channel of blessings to others, that I may know Thy grace, Thy mercy, Thy love—even as I show such to my fellow man!"

And ye may be very sure the answer comes within.

Thus, as ye apply—the answer comes. Not—by applying—do we mean a separation from the world. For even as He, ye are *in* the world but not *of* the world. But putting away the worldly things ye take hold upon the spiritual things, knowing that the worldly are but the shadows of the real.

And thus, as ye come into the light of His countenance, it maketh thy heart glad in the consciousness of *"I am Thine—Thou art mine."*

Ready for questions.

(*Q*) *What was the exact time of my physical birth?*

(A) Eight-twenty in the morning.

(*Q*) *What was the exact time of my soul birth?*

(A) Only a few breaths after the physical birth. For as has been indicated to the soul, in the experiences in the earth—how beautiful have been thy joys, yea even thy sorrows, that they have kept alive that longing for a closer communion, a closer walk with Him!

And as the soul came then with a purposefulness, that "I—even I— may be able to show forth His love among those I meet day by day," there was no tarrying. For ye are learning, ye have gained, ye may apply, *"as ye sow, so shall ye reap."*

For God is not mocked. Though man may separate himself, it is against the purposes, the will of the love of truth. And only self may separate thee from the love of the Father. For He longeth, even as thy soul crieth out in the mornings, "Holy—holy art Thou, O Lord!"

(*Q*) *If possible, what can I do to finish my earth's experience in this life?*

(A) It is ever possible. Studying to show forth the Lord's death till He come again!!

What meaneth this?

Just living those that are the fruits of the spirit; namely: peace, harmony, longsuffering, brotherly love, patience. *These*, if ye show them forth in thy life, in thy dealings with thy fellow man, grow to be what? *Truth!* In Truth ye are *free*, from what? *Earthly* toil, *earthly* cares!

These then are not just axioms, not just sayings, but *living* truths!

Ye *are* happy in His *love! Hold* fast to that!

(Q) *What is holding back my spiritual development?*

(A) Nothing holding back—as has just been given—but *self.* For know, as has been given of old, "Though I take the wings of the morning in thought and fly unto the uttermost parts of the earth, Thou art there! Though I fly into the heavenly hosts, Thou art there! Though I make my bed in hell, Thou art there!"

And as He has promised, "When ye cry unto me, I *will hear*—and answer speedily."

Nothing prevents—only self. Keep self and the shadow away. Turn thy face to the light and the shadows fall behind.

(Q) *Please explain the meaning of a light I saw on the night of June 13th-14th, and a figure that appeared in the light.*

(A) These are but the beginnings of that which may be thy experience. This followed a deep meditation, though much broke in between. But it is the fruit of not thought, but purpose, desire. For it has not entered the heart of man all the glories that have been prepared, nor all the beauties that may be experienced by those that seek His face.

These are but the signs, yea the *assurances*, that His presence abideth with thee. Know He hath promised that if ye ask, ye shall receive. Be satisfied only then with the consciousness of His presence. Who? That in Whom ye have believed—that abides with thee. For "If ye will knock, I will open—for I stand at the door and knock."

If ye will but open thy tabernacle of consciousness to allow the holy to come in and sup with thee, yea *all* the beauties of peace and harmony *are* thine; for they are the birthright of each soul. For the soul is the portion of the Maker that makes thee individual, yet with the consciousness of being one with God, the *universe*, the *love*—that which *is* beauty and harmony.

(Q) *What is the meaning of the white lightning I have seen?*

(A) That awakening that is coming. More and more as the white light comes to thee, more and more will there be the awakening. For as the lights are in the colors: In the green, healing; in the blue, trust; in the purple, strength; in the white, the light of the throne of mercy itself. Ye may never see these save ye have withheld judgment or shown mercy.

(Q) *What is my worst fault?*

(A) What is ever the worst fault of each soul? *Self—self!*

What is the meaning of self?

That the hurts, the hindrances are hurts to the self-consciousness; and these create what? Disturbing forces, and these bring about confusions and faults of every nature.

For the only sin of man is *selfishness!*

(Q) *How may it be overcome?*

(A) Just as has been given; showing mercy, showing grace, showing peace, longsuffering, brotherly love, kindness—even under the most *trying* circumstances.

For what is the gain if ye love those *only* that love thee? But to bring hope, to bring cheer, to bring joy, yea to bring a smile again to those whose face and heart are bathed in tears and in woe, is but making that divine love *shine—shine—*in thy own soul!

Then *smile*, be joyous, be glad! For the day of the Lord is at hand.

Who is thy Lord? Who is thy God?

Self? Or Him in Whom ye live and move and have thy being—that is *all* in All, God the Father, the Love—the *great* Hope, the Great Patience? These are thy *all*.

Keep in the way that is arising before thee, more and more. And as ye open thy consciousness to the Great Consciousness within, there will arise more and more the white light.

For He is the light, and the life—eternal.

TEXT OF READING 274-3 M 35

This psychic reading given by Edgar Cayce at his home on Arctic Crescent, Va. Beach, Va., this 8th day of June, 1933, in accordance with request made by self——Mr. [274], Active Member of the Ass'n for Research & Enlightenment, Inc.

PRESENT

Edgar Cayce; Gertrude Cayce, Conductor; Gladys Davis, Steno. Mildred Davis and L. B. Cayce.

READING

Time of Reading ... Street, 11:10 to 11:50 A. M. Eastern Standard Time. N.Y.C., N.Y.

(Body & enquiring mind, in regard to his mental and spiritual well-being. Mental & Spiritual reading.)

EC: Yes, we have the body, the enquiring mind, [274].

In considering the mental and spiritual welfare, this may be in a manner the correlating of that which has been given for the physical body and for the mental and imaginative body.

Then, these are the conditions that are set before the body; and as to what the body in the present does with or about that given is a matter more for self-consideration and self-appreciation.

For, mental and spiritual must of itself partake of that which has been builded in the experience of the entity in *all* its application of that which has been gained, and that is approachable to the mental forces of the body through the inner self—which is that sought, that is obtainable to the consciousness through the intuitive or the psychic influences about the body, as well as through the application of those conditions of which the body is aware within the mental being.

First, then, in the physical we find there are changes coming about that are gradually making for more satisfactory responses in an ability of the body-physical to apply that which is known in self respecting its general physical welfare in the present time.

As this ability comes about, as it is known and will be experienced by the body, the more aware and the more alive the body will be in *every* portion of its activity; or in the manifestation does it become alive; and alive means life manifesting in an expression of the spiritual influences in a material world, or the psychic influences in the physical being of an entity.

Then, in making the application of these things, we find these will build more and more to not only the *enjoyment* of life and its manifestation, but to the greater *abilities* in every sense to give out—which will become aware in the mental and material influences about the body.

We would continue, then, to make those applications of material and mechanical influences, in, of and to the body, that these physical attributes may become more and more aware of the *abilities*, the opportunities, the obligations, the effects the body may create, may present, may use, in its experience.

For these followed will make for a much nearer normal manifestation in the whole physical being.

As to the mental body, then, we have given how the mental being has—through its various experiences in the earth's plane—made use of its abilities, sometimes for weal and sometimes for woe.

These, as we have pointed out to the entity, are now presenting themselves as urges in the mental influences; so that there are particular, specific and definite attractions in certain fields, certain lines of endeavor.

Weighed with that which is the experience the mental being in the present, these now present themselves to be acted upon.

What, then, *is* the entity to do with these impulses? How may the entity know *how* to apply, how to use these impulses that arise, to the greater development in the present?

It has been pointed out to each and every entity that the entity, the soul, is a portion—an effort of the Creative influence to make aware in a manifested form in the earth or material world of *what* creative forces *are!* This is seen in the abilities of man as the representative of that influence made in the image, through its mental attribute, of that Creative Force.

Then, what should be the ideal? What should be the entity's activity, the entity's attitude, the entity's purpose, as in relation to that influence which manifests itself through an individual, that is termed (by man) the spiritual influence in his life?

To make the ideal, purpose, aim, less than an ideal presenting the concept of that Creative Force *in* a material plane is falling short, to be sure, of a purpose.

To use such an influence, desire, aim and ideal, to make for that which is satisfying the individual purposes, without respect of its *being* a manifestation of the same character of love that brought the entity into being, or that creates for the companionship and relationship that is of the spiritual influences, as it manifests in Creative Forces in a material world, is to become selfish, self-centered, purposeless, in the spiritual sense, and self-indulgent in the mental self, and must—as we have pointed out to the body, in its experiences—bring that which makes for unrest, contention, strife, and the builded influence then becomes purposeless; for it must be disappointing, for it is not founded in Life—which *is constructive* to the *whole*, not for an individual.

But when one makes the purpose, the aim, the ideal, one *with* the fruits of the spirit, then these become the activities of the entity, the mind, the body of such an one. And there is given to such those opportunities, those talents, that they may be presented more and more to the material world in the manifestations of that which makes for those fruits of harmony, contentment, peace, understanding, brotherly love; and *these* make life worthwhile.

How, then, may these be applied in self? How does one reach those attitudes that self may be made more and more selfless, that more and more the fruits of the spirit may be manifested in the life of an individual, a soul, seeking to know the light, the truth, the way, that may be manifested by such an one?

As given, in self is that seed of the spirit—in Life itself.

The issues of life in the physical body are those tenements [habitations?] of the mental and soul being of a physical body.

Then, in meditation, in prayer; not in long-facedness, not in closing self to those things about self that make for a contentment in the material things of life, but let *those* things be rather the effect and *not* the purpose of the mind!

So may one be joyous, being kind, being loving, being open-hearted, open-minded to those things wherein that in the word spoken, in the manifestation of the smile in the face, in the eye, to those that the self contacts, there is brought forth that from the hearts, the minds, the souls of those whom the entity contacts day by day!

Turn self *inward* then, at given periods, at specific times.

In the material world we find a set time, a period, for the accomplishing of, the carrying out of, the daily tasks that may add to the betterment of a commercial association in any given field.

We see definite periods set aside for the replenishing of the body with the fuels that may be consumed and assimilated by the body.

Foods of the spirit are as necessary to the mental well-being as the carnal forces of foods for the maintaining of an equilibrium in the physical body.

Hence, set a portion of self to those periods of communing with the inner self through meditation and prayer to the Giver of all good and perfect gifts; knowing there is a mediator that ever stands ready to make intercession, and He has given those promises that anywhere, any time that the soul calls, He *will* harken, He will guide.

And this communication gives what to the mental being?

As the carnal foods make for strength, physical vitality, so do the foods of the spirit make for *strength* in the Lord, strength in that Creative Force which we see so well manifested in the various ways and manners in and among men.

Be not unmindful that there is that way which brings self the awareness of His presence, God's presence, the Master's presence, and the better self that has experienced—through the eons of time—those relationships to the mental things that have presented themselves as problems, conditions, experiences; but He has promised, "I will stand in thy stead" in such conditions, if ye will but put your trust, your faith, in Him; for He *is* the way.

Then, let that mind be in thee as was in Him, and after this manner pray in the meditations:

As I open my mind, Oh Father, to Thy ways, wilt Thou ever in and show me the way Thou would have me go day by day!

Help me in all things. Make me strong in Thy might. Let the little hindrances of body, of associations, the unkindnesses in individuals, be turned more and more into an appreciation of Thy love made manifest in Thy gift to the world in the Master among men!

So let me live, so direct me in Thy ways, that my will may be Thy will, Thy ways may be my ways!

Keep all that Thou hast promised, for I look to Thee as the giver and the finisher of my soul!

In such ways as this, then, may the inner self become more and more aware of the possibilities of the body's efforts, and as these develop there is shown day by day that manner in which those whom the entity contacts—the ways in which *others*—may know the way.

Not some great deed, but rather just being kind one to another.

For, as *He* went about doing good—so may the kind word turn away wrath, so may the gentle look quicken the heart of the sad and make for the awareness that God is in His holy temple in thee; for thy body is the temple of the living God.

To present that body as a *living* ensample is but a reasonable service.

And when these things that are shown thee make for such a cloud of witnesses that His love is manifest in the earth, what manner of man should one be?

Show forth his love in thy acts. Be not unkind. Speak not harshly of anyone, for in so doing—that thou givest out, that thou sayest, must return to thee in the way thou hast given it out!

Then, the spirit saith come; the flesh is weak; the spirit is willing.

Draw nigh unto Him, He will draw nigh unto thee!

Living in Accord with Spiritual Ideals
Reading 317-7

Then what for this body, [317], with his own environ, his own soul development, would be the *ideal* manner of approach that there may be the greater blessings to those to whom the body, mind and soul would be of a service?

Know that the influence is without, but that the influence within is *influencing* and *being* influenced by the sources or powers *from* without! What is *thy* ideal? By what measuring stick would *thou,* thyself, judge the sources of information, of aid? By what *standard* dost thou judge thyself? Be not double-minded; nor use one standard for thyself and another for that which would be thy guide. Use not one standard for thy neighbor and another for thyself. For, all is *one*—and of one source. But what the self or thy guide or thy influence would do *with* that force or power should be the determining factor respecting same.

In entering, then, cleanse thyself according to that thou hast builded in thine own self. If there is to be correction in same as thine development and thine expression advances to the greater ideal, then thou wilt be directed in same.

Open thyself for instruction. Be *willing* to be used as a channel, a means for aid to others, irrespective of self. And there will come into thine experience that which will make thine psychic forces, thine psychic powers, become more and more perfect in the expression of that thou hast as thine own ideal.

It is true that some in their physical bodies are an expression of those things that will bring to man the glory and knowledge of the Father. And do not find fault with those that use same for that expression. Do not find fault. For, hast thine Maker found fault with that in nature that has altered from expression to expression its own manifestation? Art thou greater than thine Maker? Art thou a judge among men? *Who* made thee a judge, other than of thine own purposes, thine own desires?

In such an attitude may there come—if the body, mind and consciousness will set self aright respecting such an attitude—the better, the greater development, the greater aid, the greater channel for expression.

For, as there is self, there are the powers and influences without thee. Get together! Know that in cooperation with the *Divine* that is *constructive* you may be a blessing in *any* channel that is pointed out to thee, that becomes a consciousness, an awareness in thee.

Do that.

Reading 3630–2

In the application of the use of the experiences gained: be more tolerant with others. Do study closely those promises of the divine that's in the Way, and the Truth and the Light, and know deep within self that all healing of every nature must come from the divine, and the divine is within self.

For thy body is indeed the temple of the living God. Therein ye may meet Him in prayer, in meditation, in psalm singing, yea in the activities of fasting, in not only the foods but in opening the mind, the consciousness, consciously to that which may flow in from music, from prayer, those influences which may flow in from deep meditation, which may be gained in having regular periods for this shutting out from self of the voices or the sounds of nature and listening to the still small voice within.

Before that we find the entity was in that land now known as the Egyptian, when through that great period there was the consecration of individuals, their purposes and bodies, for service through activities in the Temple of Sacrifice and the Temple Beautiful.

The entity was among those who were very helpful in those periods when home establishments were brought about. And in those activities in the present, especially as may be associated with the young, may the entity find the outlet and those activities which may bring bettered conditions—physical, mental and spiritual.

As to that to which the entity may attain and how, first: Analyze self, self's beliefs, self's purposes, self's ideals and know the great ideal is set in Thou should love the Lord thy God with all thy heart, thy mind and thy soul and thy neighbor as thy self. Have ye, do ye? Apply this in thy dealings daily or in the conditions of body and in what may happen that may cause the body to be overanxious.

Then put these down (the ideals), not merely as symbols or signs in thine own mind but write them upon paper, change them as thy experience progresses.

Then study to show forth by thy activities, day by day, deeds in the body manifesting that faith in the divine, keeping self unspotted from condemning anyone.

Reading 440-8

First, as indicated, *find self*. Find what is self's ideal. And as to how high that ideal is. Does it consist of or pertains to materiality, or spirituality? Does it bespeak of self-development or selfless development for the glory of the ideal? And be sure that the ideal is rather of the spiritual. And this may become, as given, the first psychic experience of self's own inner soul, or self's own guide—as may be chosen. And do not be satisfied with a guide other than from the Throne of Grace itself! And when the self is being taught, seek a teacher. When self needs exhortation, then seek an exhorter. When self is desiring or seeking those channels that pertain to the material, or the application of material things, that spiritual lessons or spiritual truths may be brought, then *seek* such a source, such a channel for the *creative* influences. And who better may be such a guide than the Creator *of* the universe? For, He has given that "If ye will seek me ye may find me" and "I will not leave thee comfortless" but if ye are righteous in purpose, in intent, in desire, "I will bring *all things* to thine remembrance" that are needs be for thy soul, thine mind, thine body, development.

This is a promise from Him, who is able to fulfill that which has been promised to every soul that seeks His face, His ways.

Then, speak oft with thy Maker. And let thine meditation be:

Lord, use Thou me in that way, in that manner, that I—as Thy son, Thy servant—may be of the greater service to my fellow man. And may I know His biddings, Father, as Thou hast promised that if we would hear Him that we ask in His name may be ours. I claim that relationship, Father, and I seek Thy guidance day by day!

And, as the light comes, as the feelings of the understandings come— never by chance, but in His ways doth He bring to pass that way, that channel, those individuals *through* whom self may make for *soul's* development—through those things that may come to thee, do ye walk in the Way.

This, then, is the manner for self to develop, for self to know, for self to understand.

Naturally, the question arises within self, how shall I know?

In what manner will it be given me to know who is giving the information, who is speaking?

As outlined, first the answer is within self's own mental self, as to whatever is being sought.

Then in the meditation of that given in outline as a diet for the soul body, for the psychic faculties, the answer will be in the spirit. And each time, each experience when there is being sought for self as to What manner of activity or what manner or course is the right way to pursue, may it be given what manner or could thee in the same way and manner.

If the approach is through some associate, some friend, some brother that is acting in the capacity as a sign, as a guide post along the way of life, then know that thou hast been guided to that way—and ye yourself must walk that road; and that ye may not walk alone—rather with His guiding hand will the way be shown, will the way be made plain in thine endeavors.

Keep self out of the way. Stumble not over the pitfalls that arise from self's anxiety, self's indulgences or self's expression of aggrandized interests—but let thy ways be His ways. Then ye shall know the truth and the truth shall make you free.

Reading 3374-1

(Q) *Please advise me how I might best develop my soul forces?*
(A) Look to Him, and let thy prayer oft be—live it—be it:
Lord, here am I! Use Thou me in the way Thou seest I may best fulfill the purpose Thou hast for me in the earth now.

Reading 263-11

(Q) *Please give me any mental or spiritual advice that would help me at this time?*
(A) In all of thy meditations and in thy prayers, let that attitude continue to be:
Thy will, Thy purpose, not mine! Make me willing to be the channel Thou would have me to be, O Lord; that my life and my associations may be beautiful, and helpful, in the experiences of those I meet and am associated with day by day.

Reading 3416-1

(Q) *How may I best develop myself spiritually?*
(A) Through prayer and meditation. Turn ever to Him for as He has given, practice daily the love of the Christ. For as He gave, "A new commandment I give unto you, that ye love one another." Then manifest that in every way. Let everyone that you meet be happier for having met you, for having spoken to you. This ye can do by spreading joy. This is the manner to unfold, to develop. Then in thy meditation, present thyself as a willing channel, to be as the hands, as the eyes, as the voice of thy Master.

Applying Spiritual Principles in Everyday Life

Reading 826-11

(Q) *Is there any particular psychic faculty which I should develop in this experience that would enrich my daily life?*

(A) As has been indicated, this may be developed in the manner as
has been given. It is the heritage of each soul. If ye in thine own consciousness are desirous of meeting Him, thy Maker, thy Father in the
temple of thine own soul, then meditate upon Him, applying that ye
know today!

For it is in the application, not the knowledge, that the truth becomes
a part of thee.

It is not in thine body that what ye eat is thy body, but that the
body—through thy digestive self—puts *into use in* muscle, bone, blood,
tissue—yea the very blood and the very streams thorough which the
mentality flows! Thy *brain* is not thy mind, it is that which is used by thy
mind!

What then *is* thy mind? The gift of God, that is the companion with
thy soul, that is a part of same! Then if ye would develop that by its use,
by its application, it is ministering good and goodness; not for self. For
that ye give away *alone* do ye possess! For the that would have life must
give it. He that would know the faculties of the psychic force, or the
soul, must *manifest* same in the relationships to spiritual truths, spiritual
law, spiritual application.

(Q) *Please explain in detail the steps I should take in this development, in meditation, that would be most consistent with my inner self?*

(A) In whatever manner that thine own consciousness is a cleansing
of the body and of the mind, that ye may present thyself *clean* before
thyself and before thy God, *do!* Whether washing of the body with water, purging of same with oils, or surrounding same with music or incense. But *do that thy consciousness* directs thee! Not questioning! For he
that doubteth has already built his barrier!

Then, meditation upon that which is thy highest ideal within thyself,
raise the vibrations from thy lower self, thy lower consciousness through
the centers of thy body to the temple of thy mind, thy brain, thy eye
that is single in purpose; or to the glandular forces of the body as the
Single Eye.

Then, listen—listen! For it is not in the storm, not in the noise, but the
still small voice that rises within.

And let thy query ever be:

Here am I, O God, use me—send me! Do with me as Thou seest! Not my will, but

Thine—O God—be done in and through me.

These are the manners. Not that the things of the material mind are to be neglected, but remember this: It is the foolishness of God that is the wisdom of man. It is the wisdom of man misapplied that is the foolishness to God.

(Q) How may I come to a greater realization of my inner spiritual power and the relation of this power to all Creative Force?

(A) That has been given over and over again, here in this: In *applying* that ye know *today!* and tomorrow the next step is given. For it is line upon line, precept upon precept, here a little, there a little. And if ye would have thy God—yea thy better self be patient with thee, then be patient with thy study, yea thy fellow man.

For indeed as He gave, "In patience possess ye your souls."

Then, as ye are manifested before thy consciousness *in* thy consciousness, become aware of this; not only as ye see the unfoldment of life in matter as a manifestation of that force and power ye would worship as thy God, thy companion, thy Lord, yea thy *brother,* thy portion of thyself, *but* in time, in space, in patience is the heart of it all!

Reading 270-33

Then, to overcome, as has been indicated, *meditate!* Meditation means entering into the *spiritual* vitalization of the energies of the system, by *raising* those forces through the very activities of procreative actions. Read *Meditation* [A.R.E. paper which later became 1st chapter in *A Search For God,* Book I.], and apply it—*practically*—the experience of self!

(Q) Please guide me with information that will enable me to become of greater service to my fellow man.

(A) There's none better than we have given, and as may be followed by that which may be brought to the awareness of self through the *practical* application of those meditative forces that come by setting aside a definite time, a period during each day's activity when there will be the purifying of the body, as in accord with that which would make for consecrating of self in all of its efforts, all of its abilities, and entering into the holy of holies within self for that talk with thy God within thyself. These efforts on the part of any soul will bring those things that make for the greater peace and happiness and the abilities to meet those emergencies of every nature that arise within the physical and mental bodies of a living body. For then the God–forces that are the creative energies of the soul–mind will become the ruling forces in the life and in its activity in same; making for those abilities wherein any soul, any entity, may become the greater service, the greater factor in its associations with its fellow man. It is not how much one knows that counts, but how well one applies that it knows; in just being, doing, thinking, that which is pointed out to self through such constant, consistent, *practical* dependence upon the Creative Forces that have promised ever to meet one—every one—when sought. And there will come that which is for the greater development in the soul forces of such an one that seeks.

Reading 1947-3

(Q) *Please give detailed directions for the entity regarding her mental and spiritual development through meditation. Outline the steps she should take that best fit her development.*

(A) First—as was indicated to those of old—purge or purify thy body—whether this be by mental means or by ablutions, do it in that manner as to satisfy thine own conscience.

Then, enter into the holy of holies of thine own inner self; for there He hath promised to meet thee. Let thy prayer be as this:

"As I surround myself with the consciousness of the Christ-Mind, may I—in body, in purpose, in desire—be purified to become the channel through which He may *direct* me in that *He*, the Christ, would have me do;" as respecting an individual, a condition, an experience. And as ye wait on Him, the answer will come.

Then each day *live*, towards those ye meet, in the same manner as ye prayed.

(Q) *Through what method or manner should my psychic abilities be expressed?*

(A) These, as we have just indicated, will be different with varied or different individuals.

Did He teach those at the well the same as those in the mount, or by the sea? Rather as He was given utterance, so gave He to others.

As has been indicated, the entity will find there are intuitive forces aroused by these applications of these purposes and desires. To some it will be healing, cooling the brow of those who are ill. To others it will be counseling as to this or that which disturbs their mental association, their moral lives, their material concepts. To others it will be as directing them to bear *their* cross even as He. For in Him does the burden become light, and the cross easy.

Reading 3098-2

As the entity may experience in some of its moments of meditation, the finding of peace in self enables the entity to give more assurance, more help to others; just by being patient and not attempting to control or to appear overanxious.

For, according to the true law of spirit, like begets like. Thus as harmony and beauty and grace reign within the consciousness of an entity, it gives that to others—and others wonder what moved them to feel different, when no one spoke, no one even appeared to be anxious. This is the manner in which the spirit of truth operates among the children of men.

4

●

Having a Closer Walk with the Divine Through Meditation and Prayer

Spiritual Healing Becomes Possible Through Having a Closer Walk

(Note: Although focusing on prayer and spiritual healing, this reading, given to the original prayer group, describes some of the spiritual gifts that are possible by having a closer walk with the Divine.)

TEXT OF READING 281-27

This psychic reading given by Edgar Cayce at his home on Arctic Crescent, Virginia Beach, Va., this 11th day of June, 1936, in accordance with request made by those present.

PRESENT

Edgar Cayce; Gertrude Cayce, Conductor; Gladys Davis, Steno. Helen Ellington, Margaret Wilkins, Ruth LeNoir, Florence and Edith Edmonds, Esther Wynne, Hannah and Noah Miller, Ethel Parry, Myrtle Demaio, and Hugh Lynn Cayce.

READING

Time of Reading 11:55 to 12:15 Noon.

GC: You will have before you the Glad Helpers, members of which are present here, and their work and study of the subject of spiritual healing. You will give them such guidance and counsel as is needed at this time and answer the questions which will be asked.

EC: Yes, we have the group as gathered here, and their work in the spiritual healing.

Much has been given through these channels as to manners and means of individuals and as a group being of help, aid, to those who seek to know, to experience their relationships to Creative Influences as may be applied in their individual lives.

Some we would reiterate, some we would alter somewhat in its presentation.

For Truth is a growing experience in the hearts and the minds of individuals as they apply those tenets of the law in their individual experience.

The greater the understanding of the physical bodies, the greater the understanding of those conditions, those experiences that hinder individual application of spiritual laws, the greater there may be the ability of a group, of an individual, to bring aid and help and hope in the experiences of others.

Not Knowledge that may be of the nature that is as of a scientific nature from the material viewpoint, but the less an individual or a group seeks for self-exaltation the greater may be the strength of a unified meditation, a unified prayer. For prayer is a supplication not only to the Creative Forces from within but *to* the Creative Forces, *with* the Creative Forces from without. As the union of these influences and forces then moves into activity in individuals who seek through a channel for more harmony, more peace, more understanding, greater may be the influence.

For hath it not been given that they who are on the Lord's side may put ten thousand of those influences to flight that would hinder a soul seeking to know the right?

As He has given in the examples of the manners and means in which He as a man, as an active influence in a material world, went about healing those that were ill in body, in mind; so with the proper understanding, with the proper interpretation of those things that hinder, the manner in which the individual may seek, thus may the individuals, the group, those as a unified force and influence seeking to help, bring to those who seek through the channel as Glad Helpers, to those that would know His face, those promises in the lives of individuals. For He gave, which is the better, which is the easier, which is the greater, to say "thy sins be forgiven thee, or to say Arise, take up thy bed and walk?"

Healing, as has been given, whether from influences in nature that have been instilled for the benefits of man throughout his activity in a material world, or whether moved by the spirit of life itself that manifests in a consciousness of His presence abiding in and about the individual activity, is all of the same source. Whether it be in the application of those influences that would separate, as He hath given, "If thine eye offend thee, pluck it out. If thine hand offend thee, cut it off." What meaneth these? that there may be in the experience of individuals those influences that become necessary in the material world for the separation of those bodily forces that have become, as it were, entangled in the influences about the individual, the influences brought on by individual activity, influences magnified by associations in the influences and activities of an individual. These then become as those forces that He hath given thee, "Who maketh afraid?" Those that let their mind dwell upon what others may say, upon how the world looketh upon the activity, these alone become afraid. Hence as He gave to those that saw, that understood, that comprehended that He was of the Spirit, "Of myself I can do nothing, but the spirit of the Father that worketh in and through me." So may ye as individuals not of thyselves but in allowing thy minds, thy bodies, thy purposes, thy aims be guided in that direction, be a channel through which the Spirit of Truth, the Spirit of Life, the Spirit of Creative Influences or God through Christ work in thee!

These be the manners in which ye may bring help to those that seek, to those that are afraid, to those that have been overcome, to those who have stumbled, to those who have erred.

For the Spirit maketh alive. The letter killeth but the spirit maketh alive.

Keep the faith as He hath given, "That ye ask in my name, that will I do, that the Father may be glorified in thee, in me." [John 14:13]

Hence as ye ask in His name, as the Father willeth, there may be brought to bear in the experience of the individual not so much of that which satisfies the ego, that which maketh for exaltation of self, that which maketh for being wellspoken of alone; rather ask that as the Father seeth the individual hath need of. These be the manners, these be the ways, these be the means which ye as individuals, as a group, may aid others.

Just giving a loving word. For hath He not given, "He that giveth a cup of water in my name shall in no wise lose his reward"? lose that touch with the Master?

Keep ye in touch with Him in thy purpose, in thy heart, in thy mind. For He hath loved thee and hath promised that He will come and abide with thee. He will bring that to thee that will give thee the more perfect understanding of that estate He had with the Father before the world was, before those experiences in the earth. And He will bring peace, harmony, understanding, glory in thy own experience. For though the heavens and the earth may pass away, though that thou hast builded in thy material world may appear to come to naught, though thy friends may forsake thee, though the very few may be in thy own experience as faithful, yet art thou faithful? Hast thou kept the way? Thinketh thou it were easy that those kept not awake for one hour, when the cares of the world, the experiences of unjustness were being piled upon Him? When ye because of a harsh word, a seeming unjustness have turned against this or that individual, when ye have separated thyself, when ye feel a hardship against another, think of thy Master. Then ye may indeed know that His promises are sure. For He hath borne the blame of the world upon His mind, His body *in the flesh;* yet He hath promised to stand between thee and those things that would make thee afraid.

For the way is easy when ye look to Him. Be ye joyous then in the fact, in the truth, in the knowledge, in the understanding that *thy* Brother, thy Savior, would be, will be, *is* nigh unto thee when ye pray, when ye seek that help, aid, health and harmony may be in the experience of thy neighbor.

For as ye do it unto the least ye do it unto Him. For *He,* the Maker, He that hath bought each soul with the price of the knowledge that He underwent all the laws of a material world that ye might have access to Him, is the source of all thy knowledge. Can ye comprehend the heart of God, to give His loved ones? Can ye comprehend how that thy prayer may save the sick, may bring harmony? As ye are in harmony the experiences come to thee. Be not faithless.

Rather let the heart of God through Christ encompass thee. Let thy purpose, thy aim, thy desires be one with Him.

For he that hath saved a soul hath indeed covered a multitude of errors in self.

Be not discouraged then, for was He discouraged? Hath He not promised to be thy stay, thy strength? Trust ye in Him.

For while it is yet light in thy experience, work that ye may show forth thy life, thy being, thy purposes, as one with His.

That there have been in thy experience those moments, those hours of joy even as with Him in His experience, that there have been and will be those moments, those hours of sorrow, those hours as of neglect, these be the natural laws in a material world, in which man finds himself entangled in the various influences that beset him upon every side. The weaknesses of the flesh, the weaknesses of desire, the weaknesses of those influences that are as appetites that have become as cultivated forces and require and desire an individual satisfaction. Yet there be only in Him that which is the true bread of life, that true water of life, the true increase in the vine, in thy life.

Ye are His. He hath chosen thee for a carrier of good tidings to those that are sick, to those that are in sorrow, to those that are afraid. Be ye then indeed Glad Helpers in His name. Through Him much may be accomplished, realized by those of thy conscience. Meet Him oft in the temple of thy body, knowing He is the author, He is the finisher. And if thy life is disturbed, if thy heart is sad, if thy body is racked with pain, it is thine bungling of the laws that are as universal as Life itself.

Life is of God; it is through Him that ye may know, then, its purposes. And thy experiences are as given of old, "Those He loveth He chasteneth, He purgeth, that they may bring forth fruit *worthy* of thy Lord, thy Master."

Be not afraid, it is thy Lord that would guide thee, that would direct thee, in all thy ways. For He *is* the Giver of all good and perfect gifts. Pray ye the Lord.

Walking with Jesus as Guide and Master
Reading 853-9

First study to show thyself approved unto Him, being not afraid but rightly dividing the words of truth; and keeping *self* unquestioned about the things of the world.

How does this then come in the experience of the entity in the present, for learning the deep meditation—and this ability to use that which is the birthright of each and every soul?

For the *soul*-entity is in the image of the Creator.

Then we find in the material body those patterns, those manners, those means. For indeed He hath given and has purposed that no soul shall lose its way, but He hath prepared for *every* soul the ways, the means of that soul knowing that He, Jesus, the Christ, is not only the Way but is the *directing* of the individual in the daily experiences—if you walk and talk with Him.

Then for what purpose is this communication, this development of the abilities of knowing that Jesus, the man—Christ, the Lord—is with thee day by day?

That ye may exalt thyself among thy fellowman? That ye may find the easy way in the daily experiences, and know nothing of the cries of thy fellowman—seeking, seeking—that cry aloud, and long, for the Way?

Was His way easy? Would ye be greater than thy Lord?

Ye may be equal with Him, for He hath given, "Abide in me and as I abide in the Father we may be one, that the *Lord* may be glorified in the earth."

Then if it is for self-gain, for self-exaltation, for the making of the way easy, ye seek that which may turn upon thee and destroy thy very activity.

But if it is that He may be glorified in thy fellowman, then ye may know.

For as He hath given, "If ye love me, keep my commandments; and as ye abide in me, ask and it shall be given thee the *desire of thy heart!*" If that desire is in accord, in attune, in at-onement with the constructive forces of thyself, thy experiences and thy relations. For He keepeth the way, ever.

Then as the body is the temple of the living soul, it is a part and parcel of the mind that is the builder.

Then as ye open in thy meditation, first surround thyself with the thought, the prayer, the desire that Jesus, in His promises, guide thee in thy seeking.

Then ye have set yourself aright.

Then again as ye raise thy power of vibratory forces through thy body, ye give thyself in body, in mind, in purpose, in desire, into the hands, into the keeping of His purposes with thee.

And His promises are sure; and that which ye receive, that *use!* For to have an ideal, for to have a purpose, for to have knowledge and understanding without the courage and the will to use same is to become a weakling, not worthy, not able above that doubt; even as Peter when he walked on the water.

And when you see the turmoils of the earth, and when you hear the cries of those that are fearful, and when you see the elements about thee apparently in destructive forces, and ye doubt—to be sure you sink into doubt and fear and despair; unless thy purpose is ever "Here am I, Lord, use me, direct me."

In that manner then, ye may attain to that consciousness of His presence, of His abiding with thee; that these influences may become the very forces that have been and are a portion of thine experience in the earth.

And when even thy fellows appear that were a part of thyself—what must ye do?

Preach and live *Christ* to *them,* in thy consciousness! Thus ye make *their* purpose, their desire, become that they, too, may know that which lifts thee above the herd and become as one that seeks to know His way!

Then, in thy material application, just make thy desire, thy purpose ever, one with Him.

Study then—not as by rote—that as begins like this: "I go to prepare a place for you, that where I am there ye may be also; for in my father's house are many mansions. Were it not so I would have told you. Ask and ye shall receive."

Study then, first, the 14th, 15th, 16th and 17th of John. *Apply* them, as "This is Jesus speaking to [853]—*speaking!*"

What is thy answer? "I am ready, Lord." Or, "As soon as I get this done, I'll try."

These ye must answer within thyself.

For the will of each entity, of each soul, is that which individualizes it, that makes it aware of itself; and as to how this is used makes thee indeed a child of God.

He hath not willed that ye should perish, that ye should want, that ye would not know Him. What have *ye* willed? What is thy way? What is thy desire?

It becomes then so simple that the simplicity becomes the complexness of the daily life.

Yet as ye enter into thy temple, where He hath promised to meet thee, *cleanse* thyself in body, in mind, in the manner as seemeth good to thee—whether washed with water, washed with blood, or with incense, or in music, or in the din of the city or in the quiet of the forest. For though ye take the wings of the morning and fly to the utmost parts of heaven, ye will find Him there; and though ye sink to the depths of hell ye will find Him there; and He hath promised, and as He hath given, "Though the heavens and the earth fail, and though they pass away, My word and my promise shall not pass away." And His promise has been, "When ye *call* I will *hear!*"

These are thine. These are thy possibilities, these are thy abilities. What will ye do with them?

Reading 1158-9

In giving further interpretations of those records as we find in the experience of the entity, and their application in the present, it is very well, very befitting that such should come at a season or time when there were the experiences of the entity as the sister of the risen Lord; that there may be in the experience of the entity those practical experiences and practical applications.

For as has been intimated, each soul that has named the Name and who keeps in the Way may know, may hear, may see, may have a consciousness of that *entity*; yea, the consciousness of being at an at-onement with Jesus, the Christ.

Not merely as a condition, not merely what may be termed in the universal sense as being at an at-onement in the Christ Consciousness (which is a condition, an experience, an activity), but that it may be fulfilled even as He has given in His promises; "Abide in me and I in thee, and I in the Father, that we may be One, even as I and the Father are One; that I may bring to remembrance thy remembrance from the book of thine own records *all* that has been from the foundations of the earth!"

Then as each soul meditates, uses, applies, consciously, His promises, and makes them its own, then indeed may it again walk and talk with Him.

Reading 2533-4

(Q) Outline additional comprehensive instructions that will enable this entity to meditate on any problem that may arise and get the solution.

(A) As has been indicated so oft for others, as well as for this entity—ye as an individual are made in the image of the Creator. Ye are, as an individual, remembered by Him—which is demonstrated in thy awareness of thy ability, thy consciousness in the present of being alive and conscious of the faults and the failures of thy fellow man about you, and of thine own shortcomings in meeting or fulfilling all of thine own ideals as to the relationship an individual soul-entity should bear to the Creative Forces or God.

Yet ye realize the possibilities, the opportunities that lie latent within. For, as was given of old—Say not as to who will descend from heaven that ye may have a message, for Lo, it is in thine own heart. For, thy body is indeed the temple of the living God. There He—as all knowledge, all undertakings, all wisdom, all understanding—may commune with thee, if ye but give that opportunity, that force an opportunity to open thine heart, thine mind, thy understanding, to His presence.

Ye believe, and ye know, and ye understand, that His Son, thy Brother, entered into the flesh that ye might have not only that promise of old that man has gotten so far from, but that ye might today have an advocate with the Father; that ye might know not only that thine own angel of thyself, what thou hast been, stands ever as the evidence of thy consciousness, thy awareness, thy presence in the throne of the Father, but that thy Brother, thy Representative, thy Friend, stands ever ready to intercede for thee. And, as He hath given, He stands continually at the door of thy consciousness, of thy heart. If ye will open, He will enter.

How do ye open? By attuning, turning thy thought, thy purpose, thy desire to be at an at-onement with Him. The atonement has been offered. Thus ye have that assurance that as ye seek His face He will come and abide.

Thus, as ye seek for any purpose—worthy or unworthy—these will be made known to thee, and the course thou shouldst pursue. In this, even as He:

"Not my will, Lord, but Thine be done in me, through me, day by day. May I ever be the channel that may bring to my fellow man that awareness of Thy love—by the manner in which I, myself, treat my fellow man day by day; knowing, in my own heart and mind, that inasmuch as or in the manner I treat my brother, here, I am treating my brother who stands in my stead before Thy throne."

Reading 272-8

(Q) Regarding mental and spiritual: What may be done to assist in the coming of the Awakening to me?

(A) As indicated, do not be overanxious; yet be consistent and persistent in thy studies and in the application of self in the light of that which has been given thee. If thou wilt do the acts that will bring into thine experience day by day the fruits of the spirit to, for and with thy fellow man, then the same will be magnified and glorified in thee; and thou wilt find that more and more He will walk and talk with thee in thy meditations and thy prayers. For, He is willing, yet He *waits* thy bidding and thy activity. Be not overcome with remorse nor anxiety, nor be overzealous; but be ye joyous in the praise of thy Father through His Son, the Christ.

(Q) How may my mind and body be cleansed for meditation?

(A) No better way than that we have given. Cleanse first thy body, in making preparation for each day's meditation, in the way or manner that seemeth well unto thee. Then open thine self that the glory of the Father through the promises in the Christ may be magnified in thine inner self. Study well those promises that are thine in the 14th, 15th, 16th, and 17th chapters of John in the King James Version, and know that these refer to thee. In each line, in each verse, see self receiving those promises, those blessings that He has promised. For, as He gave, He that receiveth a prophet in the name of a prophet receives a prophet's reward. Let not thine heart be troubled, neither let it be afraid.

(Q) *How may I assist in helping the doors of light to be opened to me?*

(A) Do not try to assist self, but rather smile upon those that are downhearted and sad; lift the load from those that find theirs too heavy to bear, in gentleness, in kindness, in long-suffering, in patience, in mercy, in brotherly love. And as ye show forth these to thy fellow man, the ways and the gates of glory open before thee. Who hath called on the Lord; they that are weighted with the cares of the earth, those whose souls seek the solace of His blessings and the glory of His message and promises to men? They that are in such an attitude find the gates, the doors, ajar.

(Q) *May I know divine love?*

(A) As ye see it expressed in the lives about thee, ye may know it and *have* it as thine own. As ye show forth the attributes of the Father, in manifesting love and mercy and grace and patience and long-suffering, so do ye see the beauties of divine love. So do ye see it expressed in the lives of thy fellow man. So do ye find these conditions in thy experience. If ye would have friends, be *friendly* to those about thee! If ye would know the Father, then manifest Him in thy walks and thy talks with thy fellow man. If ye would have divine love, show love and mercy and patience to thy fellow man in every walk of life.

For, Life itself in all its forms is the manifestation of that the Father would shed upon the sons and daughters of men that glory in Him. Be happy and glad. Smile though the heavens fall. And though thy best friend deceive thee, and though thine own loved ones forsake thee; when they forsake thee thy Father, thy God, will take thee up.

Reading 262–56

(Q) [993]: *Please interpret fully my experience of about 10 days ago regarding the Master walking with someone in the garden.*

(A) In the meditation were the experiences of the awareness of that which separated itself (This, to be sure, is given in light of the lesson here, you see). The separation of light from the source of light, that manifested itself in the material, the mental and the spiritual world. The walking in the garden represents the figure of the oneness of light, the oneness of purpose, the closeness of that source of light to those that seek to know the way as He would have each one go.

Hence more and more there may come to those that seek the experiences that to them represent or give the better interpretation and understanding of that they seek in the study of the way He, the Master, would have them go.

(Q) [69]: *What is the best time of day for me to seek greater attunement with the Infinite in obtaining something for the lesson?*

(A) It is the material experience of the entity that this is changeable. At some periods it may be in the quietness even of the nighttime, and at others even when the hands are the busiest—or the mind there comes the awareness of the activity in the direction of the mental being, to the studies of this lesson or this thought.

Hence, as He has given, be constant in prayer, be watchful, and be mindful of that which may be obtained when the self is in attune, when there is felt, seen, heard the expressions of that which may come over, in, or through the mental being.

Reading 1173–10

But let the theme of the mental body ever be *Jesus*, the Savior, the merciful companion to those who seek to know God's way with men. For He *is* that friend that would ever guide, direct and *accompany* thee, in trials, temptations, in thy joys as well as sorrows.

So, take Him with thee as thy companion in thy studies, in thy preparations, in thy thoughts of others, in thy *joys*. For would ye as a friend to man hear only sorrow as each and every word of those that sought thee! The heart of God in the Christ seeks the *joy*; as He did in giving His Son that we might know Him the better.

Then, hold fast to that which is good in thy activities day by day; and ye will find life as abundant, as purposeful, even as He.

For He *is* the light, the guide, to all.

Finding At-One-ment and the Divine Within
Reading 281–24

(Q) *Is it possible to give any advice as to how an individual may raise his own vibrations, or whatever may be necessary, to effect a self-cure?*

(A) By raising that attunement of self to the spirit within, that is of the soul—body—about which we have been speaking.

Oft in those conditions where necessary ye have seen produced within a body unusual or abnormal strength, either for physical or mental activity. From whence arose such? *Who* hath given thee power? Within what live ye? *What* is Life? Is it the *attuning* of self, then, to same. *How?*

As the body–physical is purified, as the mental body is made wholly at-one with purification or purity, with the life and light within itself, healing comes, strength comes, power comes.

So may an individual effect a healing, through meditation, through attuning not just a side of the mind nor a portion of the body but the whole, to that at-oneness with the spiritual forces within, the gift of the life–force within each body.

For (aside, please), when matter comes into being, what has taken place? The Spirit ye worship as God has *moved* in space and in time to make for that which gives its expression; perhaps as wheat, as corn, as flesh, as whatever may be the movement in that ye call time and space.

Then *making* self in an at-onement with that Creative Force brings what? That necessary for the activity which has been set in motion and has become manifested to be in accord *with* that First Cause.

Hence do we find it becomes necessary that ye speak, ye act, that way. For whosoever cometh to offer to self, or to make an offering to the throne of mercy or grace, and speaketh unkind of his brother, is only partially awake or aware.

For that which has brought distraughtness, distress, disease in the earth, or in manifestation, is transgression of the law.

Reading 922–1

There is that access, then, that way, to the Throne of grace, of mercy, of peace, of understanding, within thine own self. For He has promised to meet thee in thine own temple, in thine own body, through thine own mind. And as He has given of old, as He has made manifest in the flesh, as He has spoken to thee and to thy fellow man again and again, consecrate your mind, your body; purge same in a manner that *to thee* in thine own consciousness has made and does make thee as receiving thy Lord, thy God! And then enter into the holy of holies, within thine own consciousness; turn within; see what has prompted thee. And He has promised to meet thee there. And there *shall* it be *told* thee from within the steps thou shouldst take day by day, step by step. Not that some great exploit, some great manner of change should come within thine body, thine mind, but line upon line, precept upon precept, here a little, there a little. For it is, as He has given, not the knowledge alone but the practical application—in thine daily experience with thy fellow man—that counts. Not that one seeks out this, that or the other manner, or the other channel; for lo, He is within thine own self—yet without, that He may guide, *guard*, direct thy ways day by day! It is just in *living* those things in the material manner that are the fruits of the Spirit, that bring with them their reward—which maketh for the understanding within thee: Love ye one another; show forth gentleness, kindness; speak softly, even to those that are harsh; upbraid not; condemn not; be long-suffering. Be patient, even with thine own self; not as some men count patience, but as an activative principle, as an activative experience in thine own self. For as the Master of Masters has said; *in patience* possess ye, do ye become aware of, thine own soul! See, know, feel, understand that thy body is but the shell, the shadow, the encasement of thy soul; with thy mind that is both spiritual and material, that partakes of heaven—yea, and of hell also. For as He has given, as heaven is His home and earth His footstool, "as ye are in me and I in thee and I in the Father," so abide ye; that ye may know. Not that, then, which maketh afraid. Not that which is of fear. Not that which is of trembling. But the *love*, the peace, the patience, the mercy, that casteth out fear; the patience that turneth away wrath; the mercy that doeth good even unto those that speak evil of thee, who despitefully use thee, who say unkind things about thee. Speak gently. These make for that within self which brings the awareness such that thy face, thy body, *shines* even as a light unto Him. For if He abides with thee, *who* can make thee afraid?

Reading 1151–14

And know, O son of man, thy prayers, thy meditations, rise as a sweet incense before the throne of mercy and peace and grace!

Thy efforts in the behalf of thy fellow man *will* not, *do not* go unheard; nor will they be unrewarded in thy daily life.

Let then peace, mercy and judgement rest with thee; knowing that the Father is in His holy temple within thee—and that as ye measure to others, so does it return to thee.

Rail not on those who would despitefully use thee, or attempt to misconstrue thy efforts! For He, thy Lord, thy Guide, will sustain thee—if ye will carry the whole matter to Him!

Rememberest thou how ye walked by the way and were troubled as to what would befall those of thy own countrymen, as well as those of the household of Him with Whom ye walked? and how He quieted thy fears by reminding thee that for this purpose came He into the earth?

And though it might appear that the day was spent, and the truths He had presented before those of the land were closed, did He not *confirm* in thy own consciousness the fact that those things which had been spoken and done as it were in the secret place would be proclaimed openly? and thus come as the leaven—as was given of old, by all the teachers—that would leaven the whole lump? and become the judgements of those in every phase and walk of life, by which *man* would judge his dealings with his fellow man?

Hold fast to that, O Friend! For that is thy strength; that is thy bulwark of safety!

Reading 531-5

. . . His strength and power is sufficient, and that in whatsoever ye may find constructive forces manifesting, He is there. For, as has been said of old: "If I take the wings of the morning to fly into the utmost parts of the earth, He is there. Though I descend into the bowels of the earth, or into the depths of the sea, He is there. Though I make my bed in hell, He is *there*." That promise, "When ye call I will hear, for I am closer than thy hand, closer than thy inner self." *Open* thy heart, thy mind, that He may enter in.

Reading 899-1

In giving that as may be helpful to a physical body that has grown in the mental and in the physical week, and often weary of the material surroundings, it is well that those who have the ministrations and those that would aid know that the greater help, the greater aid that may be brought to one so soul-weary is the *unified* expression of that Christ-Consciousness which may arise within the body through the awareness of that divinity in all. This may bring the greater joy, the greater peace, the greater harmony in this soul's, this entity's experience in the present.

Reading 849-17

(Q) *What can the entity do to bring himself more nearly and deeply into the spiritual attunement which he seeks?*

(A) Hold *fast* to that which has prompted thee, which has directed thee, that has held thee close! For as has been indicated, the more oft the entity has entered, does enter, into the deeper communion with self, in that temple of thine own body where He has promised to meet thee! For indeed thy body is the temple of the living God, and thou—keeping it holy, swept clean from those influences that would make for the offering of strange fires or that would make for those experiences that would bring into the minds and hearts of others doubts or fears—may be drawn closer and closer to Him.

For He stands ever at the door of thy conscience; He stands ever as a lamp to thy feet, as a light to the pathway. And unless ye shatter same by the greater material desire, He will lead the way.

Reading 267-1

(Q) *Please explain what was meant by seeking universal source as contact for helping self and others?*

(A) Seeking the Spirit, or the *continuity* of Life *within* self, which is the gift of the Creative Force in the experience of every entity!

(Q) *Outline in detail how I could go about the development of self to make this possible in the highest manner?*

(A) By meditation and prayer in the name of that held as highest to the influences to the Throne itself; for in the *training* of the inner self may those *attunements* come—even as there is seen manifested in the mental experience those intonations that make for the influences upon the impulses, the influences upon the inner life, are controlled by the gentler, the more delicate tones, rather than the harsh.

Living in Accord with Divine Will

Reading 2823-3

(Q) How can I increase my awareness of the universal God Force, to enable me to become more of a blessing to my associates?

(A) As just indicated. In that attuning of body, mind and soul to those onenesses of purpose, as they each give expression of those influences manifested in the Godhead.

(Q) Please give instructions on meditation.

(A) For this body—not for everybody—odors would have much to do with the ability of the entity to meditate. For, the entity in the experiences through the Temple of Sacrifice became greatly attuned through the sense of smell, for the activities were upon the olfactory nerves and muscles of the body itself. For there the protuberances were taken away.

As to the manner of meditation, then: Begin with that which is oriental in its nature—oriental incense. Let the mind become, as it were, attuned to such by the humming, producing those sounds of o-o-o-ah-ah-umm-o-o-o; not as to become monotonous, but "feel" the essence of the incense through the body-forces in its motion of body. This will open the kundalini forces of the body. Then direct same to be a blessing to others. These arise from the creative center of the body itself, and as they go through the various centers direct same; else they may become greater disturbing than helpful. Surround self ever with that purpose, "Not my will, O God, but Thine be done, ever," and the entity will gain vision, perception and—most of all—judgment."

Reading 262-64

(Q) [379]: How can we discriminate between selfish and unselfish desires?

(A) As to what has motivated and does motivate the desire. If it is for the self, or for the glorification of the Christ Consciousness in thine experience. That this or that may appear to self as being well, if such and such an experience were thine own. But, as has been given, each soul may find in self an answer to that it seeks or desires to *know* from what source it (the desire) *has* originated, or is in its impelling force. First ask self in the physical consciousness, and answer—and find an answer—yes or no.

Then enter into the inner self through meditation and prayer, and seek the answer there; for "My Spirit beareth witness with thy spirit as to whether thou art the sons of God or not," in thine activity, thine desire, thine purposes, thine aims.

(Q) [303]: *What should I do in order to bring into material manifestation my desires? Are not physical needs in life spiritual in essence?*

(A) If the desires for the physical things in life are *spiritualized*, they are indeed then as necessary as the higher motivative force in spiritual things. But who is the judge? He that is the Giver of all good and perfect gifts. Even as He prayed, "Father, let this cup pass from me, but *Thy* will—not mine—be done." Again and again do we see in this the manifestation of the flesh warring with the spiritual life itself. And we are to be in that position in our desires that His pattern, His life, is the pattern for our lives. Seek ye ever, but *Thy will, O God, be done in me, through me, as Thou seest; for the desire of my heart is that I may be the channel of blessings to others in the ways and manners Thou seest; not my way, O Lord, but Thy way.*

Reading 2072-14

(Q) *How can one be sure that a decision is in accordance with God's will?*

(A) As indicated here before. Ask self in the own conscious self, "Shall I do this or not?" The voice will answer within. Then meditate, ask the same, Yes or No. You may be very sure if thine own conscious self and the divine self is in accord, you are truly in that activity indicated, "My spirit beareth witness with thy spirit." You can't get far wrong in following the word, as ye call the word of God.

(Q) *What present printed version of the Bible gives the nearest to the true meaning of both the new and old Testaments?*

(A) The nearest true version for the entity is that ye apply of whatever version ye read, in your life. It isn't that ye learn from anyone. Ye only may have the direction. The learning, the teaching is within self. For where hath He promised to meet thee? Within the temple! Where is that temple? Within! Where is heaven or earth? Within! Meet thy Savior there. For He hath promised, "I stand at the door—open. If ye open, I will enter and sup with thee." Again, "If ye will open I will come in—and I and the Father will abide with thee."

There have been many versions of that which was purposed to have been written, and has been changed from all of those versions—but remember that the whole gospel of Jesus Christ is: "Thou shalt love the Lord thy God with all thy mind, thy heart and thy body; and thy neighbor as thyself." Do this and thou shalt have eternal life. The rest of the book is trying to describe that. It is the same in any language, in any version.

Reading 2174-3

(Q) How may I know when the will to a course of action is justifiable, or when I am forcing my own personal will which may lead to inaction which is equally unjustifiable?

(A) By the listening within—there is the answer. For, the answer to every problem, the answer to know His way, is ever within—the answering within to that real desire, that real purpose which motivates activity in the individual.

These appear at times to become contradictory, of course; but know—as the illustration has been used here—attunement, atonement and at-onement are *one;* just as the inner self is that portion of the infinite, while the self-will or personality is ever at war with the infinite within—for the lack of what may be called stamina, faith, patience or what not. Yet each entity, each soul, knows within when it is in an at-onement.

Reading 696-3

Give, then, in broader fields of activity, in *every* channel where those that are seeking may find; that are wandering, that are lame in body, lame in mind, halt in their manner of expression, that are blind to the beauties in their own household, their own hearts, their own minds. These thou may awaken in all thy fields. And as ye do, greater is thy vision—and He will guide thee, for He hath given His angels charge concerning those that seek to be a channel of blessing to their fellowman; that purge their hearts, their bodies, of every selfish motive and give the Christ—*crucified, glorified*—a place in its stead.

Personal Affirmations

Reading 165-21

Then, let thy purpose be, let thy prayer, thy meditation, be more and more, "I am Thine, O Lord; use Thou me more and more as a channel of blessing to my fellow man; in *Thy* way, O Lord, *not* my way!"

Reading 1151–9

Let thy meditation, thy deeper counsel with thy inner self be ever:

"Open thou my mind and heart, O God, to the needs of my fellow man: and help me in considering such to know that I—as thy servant, as thy child—may show thy love, as was shown in Him—who so well demonstrated much that seemeth turmoil must come about.

"But keeping the face to the light, and the activities of the heart and the purposes of the mind and *soul* to do *right*, will bring, does bring, the consciousness of *thy* directing influence."

Reading 1472–1

(Q) Can you tell me anything of the activity and development of my son, the entity known in this life as [...] who died at the age of 13?

(A) As has been given thee, let Him, the Way, the Life, reveal this to thee in thine *own* meditation. He is near at hand.

If thine eyes will be opened, if thy purposes will be set in the service, in the patience of love, He may reveal—as given—*all* things to thee.

Let thy deeper meditation be, in thine own way, but as these thoughts:

Lord, my Lord, my God! Thy handmaid seeks light and understanding! Open to my mind, my heart, my purpose, that which I may use in my daily service, my daily contacts, that will be more and more expressive of Thy love to the children of men.

Reading 3198–1

For, He has given "Who is my mother, my brother, my sister? They that do the will of the Father." May the entity then ever have as its prayer:

Here am I, Lord! Use me in that capacity in which the world may know of Thee in a greater, and in a better light or application.

Reading 544–1

Draw near to Him, He will draw near to thee. Let thy prayer in the meditations thou makest from day to day be: *Use me, O Father, as Thou seest fit just for today. Build that in me that will enable me to see the beauties in nature, in the earth, in my fellow man, and thus worship Thee and glorify Thee the more in this experience.*

Reading 307-15

(Q) Please give me an affirmation that will help me in carrying out the work that I hope to do.

(A) Father, God! in Thy promises—through Jesus, the Christ—I come seeking Thy guidance, Thy help.

As I open the door of my own consciousness to the consciousness of the Christ-spirit, direct me—in being, filling, that place, that purpose Thou hast and dost desire that I fill in this experience.

This I ask in the name of Him in whom I have believed.

Reading 361-11

(Q) Please give me an affirmation?

(A) Lord, here am I! Use me, in the manner and the way Thou seest that I may best manifest Thee in the earth! Let my going in, my coming out, be acceptable in Thy sight day by day. And may I ever live, act, think, that what I do and say will be in keeping with Thy will.

Reading 688-4

Live again those days. As ye would term them, live again rather the experiences; each giving this:

Not my will but Thine, O Lord, be done in and through me this day, each day: that there may be a realization of that Thou hast for us as Thy children to do in this earth of Thine. Let our days as Thou seest we may use them for Thy purposes be as Thou would have them be: each making for those concessions, for those understandings. We know our weaknesses: these we do not deny but these we overcome, O God, in Thee! For Thou art might, Thou art strength, Thou art love! Ourselves we will put away. Thee, O Lord, we magnify before Thy children!

5

●

A Focus on Prayer and Spiritual Healing

Insights on Prayer Given to the Original Prayer Group

(Note: Because of the focus of the prayer group readings, a number of excerpts from the "281 series" have been included in this section.)

Reading 281-13

As it has been defined or given in an illustrated manner by the Great Teacher, prayer is the *making* of one's conscious self more in at-tune with the spiritual forces that may manifest in a material world, and is *ordinarily* given as a *cooperative* experience of *many* individuals when all are asked to come in one accord and one mind; or, as was illustrated by:

Be not as the Pharisees, who love to be seen of men, who make long dissertation or prayer to be heard of men. They *immediately* have their reward in the physical-mental mind.

Be rather as he that entered the temple and not so much as lifting his eyes, smote his breast and said, "God be merciful to me a sinner!"

Which man was justified, this man or he that stood to be seen of men and thanked God he was not as other men, that he paid his tithes, that he did the services required in the temple, that he stood in awe of no one, he was not even as this heathen who in an uncouth manner, not with washed hands, not with shaven face attempted to reach the throne of grace?

Here we have drawn for us a comparison in prayer: That which may be the pouring out of the personality of the individual, or a group who enter in for the purpose of either outward show to be seen of men; or that enter in even as in the closet of one's inner self and pours out self that the inner man may be filled with the Spirit of the Father in His merciful kindness to men.

Now draw the comparisons for meditation: Meditation, then, is prayer, but is prayer from *within* the *inner* self, and partakes not only of the physical inner man but the soul that is aroused by the spirit of man from within.

Well, that we consider this from *individual* interpretation, as well as from group interpretation; or individual meditation and group meditation.

As has been given, there are *definite* conditions that arise from within the inner man when an individual enters into true or deep meditation. A physical condition happens, a physical activity takes place! Acting through what? Through that man has chosen to call the imaginative or the impulsive, and the sources of impulse are aroused by the shutting out of thought pertaining to activities or attributes of the carnal forces of man. That is true whether we are considering it from the group standpoint or the individual. Then, changes naturally take place when there is the arousing of that stimuli *within* the individual that has within it the seat of the soul's dwelling, within the individual body of the entity or man, and then this partakes of the individuality rather than the personality.

If there has been set the mark (mark meaning here the image that is raised by the individual in its imaginative and impulse force) such that it takes the form of the ideal the individual is holding as its standard to be raised to, within the individual as well as to all forces and powers that are magnified or to be magnified in the world from without, *then* the individual (or the image) bears the mark of the Lamb, or the Christ, or the Holy One, or the Son, or any of the names we may have given to that which *enables* the individual to enter *through it* into the very presence of that which is the creative force from within itself—see?

Some have so overshadowed themselves by abuses of the mental attributes of the body as to make scars, rather than the mark, so that only an imperfect image may be raised within themselves that may rise no higher than the arousing of the carnal desires within the individual body. We are speaking individually, of course; we haven't raised it to where it may be disseminated, for remember it rises from the glands known in the body as the lyden, or to the lyden [Leydig] and through the reproductive forces themselves, which are the very essence of Life itself within an individual—see? for these functionings never reach that position or place that they do not continue to secrete that which makes for virility to an individual physical body. Now we are speaking of conditions from without and from within!

The spirit and the soul is within its encasement, or its temple within the body of the individual—see? With the arousing then of this image, it rises along that which is known as the Appian Way, or the pineal center, to the base of the *brain,* that it may be disseminated to those centers that give activity to the whole of the mental and physical being. It rises then to the hidden eye in the center of the brain system, or is felt in the forefront of the head, or in the place just above the real face—or bridge of nose, see?

Do not be confused by the terms that we are necessarily using to give the exact location of the activities of these conditions within the individuals, that we may make this clarified for individuals.

Reading 281-9

GC: You will have before you the members of the healing group present in this room, who seek advice and guidance from the Master, that they may properly carry on His work in decency and order. You will answer the questions asked.

EC: Yes, we have the members of the healing group as gathered here, as a group and as individuals.

In seeking for advice and counsel, well that each take stock of themselves as related to the activities that would be brought about in the minds and hearts of those they would aid. In unison of purpose is their strength. In the prayer of those that would aid comes strength *with* that unison of purpose in Him. As there come those periods when those

seeking are aided, give thanks! Are there those periods when those seeking falter, look within—and find that in self that would be changed,
finding the fault rather in self than in others; for let each have this as
their guide, "Others may do as they may, but for me I will serve the
living God." *Through* the promises in Him that gave, "What ye ask in my
name that will the Father give you, that I may be glorified in you."
Ready for questions.

*(Q) Why have our efforts on behalf of [543] not borne fruit, [See 543-18 Reports]
as we were told through the reading that whatsoever we ask in His name shall be
done in these bodies?*

(A) This should also be judged in each one's *own* way, in behalf of
each individual. This is a test, as it were, in self—as to whether there is
being kept that which has been promised. Be not overcome by failures
in anyone's behalf, for good is accomplished in each individual prayer
that may be sought by any, and in unison is the strength made more
secure in Him. Keep faithful. Be in earnest. Be sincere in self and in that
sought. More and more will the aid come, as there is added to thine
own self those of love, and patience, and charity, and long–suffering. So
will there be awakened that that makes for the unison of strength for
those that each seek to aid. Be not weary in well doing, for *much* has
been accomplished here, much has been relieved, that will bear fruits—
some forty, some sixty, some an hundred–fold.

(Q) Why did [2155] improve so much at first and then go back?

(A) Question not the powers that give or take, for all power is of one
source—and He has mercy upon whom He will have mercy. Each as
they seek to give the aid, the strength, the power of the Christ Consciousness in the minds and hearts of those who minister with and for
the body, gain themselves, add strength and power to those so laboring
in body and mind, and aid the consciousness of the body being attempted to be aided—giving more ease, more strength to endure. Be not
slothful, nor questioning, nor yet doubting, for "As ye sow, so shall ye
reap." Heaven and earth will pass away. *His* power, His word, His promise, endures forever. That that called time seems or appears to be the
factor that intervenes should not make anyone weary or tired, for he or
she that endures unto the end shall receive that crown, that mark
wherein each recognize themselves to be set apart for a purpose in His

name. Be faithful—every one!

(Q) *What is now necessary for this body?*

(A) Keep on keeping on. Be cheerful, knowing that as He sees fit, so will He give. Keep on working with, for, toward, the more perfect understanding—each and every one.

(Q) *Please differentiate the difference in that we are told to pray for others, whilst again we are told there must be the desire on the part of the one to be, wanting to be, helped or healed?*

(A) The prayer for others is as the defense against influences that would hinder. The prayer and meditation—and the unison of purpose for healing—is as against an offense committed in the body to be overcome, or made every whit whole by His cleansing, forgiving, His life giving power. Hence the closer the union of purpose makes that as *He* gave, "thy *faith* has made thee whole." Whether easier to say, "thy sins be forgiven", or "Take up thy bed and walk"? The forgiveness, the cleansing, is in Him. Union of purpose for the offensive, or offenses. The defense—rather as the calling of *all* powers as witness of the position.

(Q) *Are the letters we are sending out touching the minds, the hearts, the souls, of those to whom they are being sent? If not, how can they be improved?*

(A) These are well at present. As the faith grows, so may the changes be made as necessary to meet the conditions as they arise from time to time. Press and impress each more and more in the individuality and the power of that that must bring the cleansing, the faith, the hope, in the minds, the hearts, the souls, and that the trust must be in *Him*, not *in* the group! The group is only lending their power, their ability, to make more aware the needs of each individual so seeking of that power! for He hath knowledge of that we have need of before we ask, but "Ask and ye shall receive." As ye know to give gifts of love, mercy, patience, with thine fellow man, even though they wrong thee in act or word, how much *more* doth thy heavenly Father give to them that ask Him. Let thine purpose be in expressing, in manifesting, His power. All praises give unto Him! Not in what I did, we did, or the other! The praise, the power, is in Him.

(Q) *Is the corrected blank I hold in my hand alright, or would you suggest any change?*

(A) Do for the present, as given—with the letter.

(Q) Is our work properly outlined at present to bring the best results?

(A) Keep on. Pray oft. Live right.

(Q) [993]: If the spoken word is stronger than thought, why is it I prefer to use the silent meditation?

(A) In each, as has been given in Vibration, there is the sounding, as it were, of those elements as manifest of the spirit in the material activity in each individual. So in self, no fault may be found that this becomes a higher vibration to self than were the word spoken. Neither does it change the fact that to the more individuals it is true that the spoken word makes a higher vibration. Just the condition or attunement of self. Don't find fault, or try to be like someone else—or try to have someone else be like you. Be like Him—all of you!

(Q) Is there any individual advice I need at this time as a member of the group?

(A) Keep on being, thinking, growing, wanting to be, more like Him.

TEXT OF READING 281-60

This psychic reading given by Edgar Cayce at the office of the Association, Arctic Crescent, Virginia Beach, Va., this 3rd day of February, 1942, in accordance with request made by approximately two hundred members of the Ass'n for Research & Enlightenment, Inc., who responded to his request to pray with him for divine guidance.

PRESENT

Edgar Cayce; Gertrude Cayce, Conductor; Gladys Davis, Steno. Esther Wynne, Florence Edmonds, Helen Ellington, Helen Godfrey, Ruth Denney and Hugh Lynn Cayce.

READING

Time of Reading 11:00 to 11:20 A. M. Eastern Standard Time.

GC: You will have before you the enquiring minds, the purposes of all those who have signified their desire to join Edgar Cayce a few minutes each day in prayer for divine guidance. You will advise these individuals what their attitude should be in the present world turmoil and how they should proceed in order to be of the greater service, as a group and as individuals. You will also advise the best time for meditation and the affirmation or prayer that should be used.

EC: Let all those who have signified their willingness to look to God for guidance know that God has remembered them. That they are conscious of being alive, with the abilities to hate and love, should indicate this to them.

Let each individual know that it came into life with a purpose from God. Let each individual know that it is as a harp upon which the breath of God would play.

While all may not be as prophets or as preachers, neither may all stand in the halls of learning as directors of men, know that you each have your part to do.

That God hath so willed that man should be free to choose should indicate for each individual his relationship to God, that may only be manifested in the manner the individual treats his fellow man.

All are aware that selfishness causes many to be downtrodden, living in hovels; that greed, as is being manifested, would make slaves of thy fellow man. Yet each individual as an individual, and as a group, may fulfill those words, "He stood between the living and the dead and the plague was stayed."

Thus each individual is alive unto God or dead unto self.

As to the periods—as near as practical, let there be unison of purpose. Early in the morning call unto thy God, and in the evening forget not His love nor His benefits.

Then, at that period when ye each are first aware, as ye awake, be *still* a moment and know that the Lord is God. Ask that ye be guided, *this* day, to so live that ye may stand between the living and the dead.

In the evening as ye sit at meat, be *still* a moment. For there is greater power in being still before thy God than in much speaking. Again give thanks for the day and its opportunities.

And so may ye, as seekers for divine guidance, be uplifted; and thus may ye hasten the day when war will be no more.

We are through for the present.

Reading 281-2

(Q) Please outline a group meditation for us which will aid us in being of aid to others.

(A) Our Father who art in heaven, *hear* our pleading for one of thine children, who in weakness has erred and seeks thy face! Mercy, O God, to us all, through Him who promised what we ask in *His* name will be done in this body!

(Q) *What times would be best for our periods of meditation in which we seek to give aid to others?*

(A) Early in the morning, late in the evening. Or seven in the morning, six in the evening.

(Q) *What connection must be established with those we are trying to help?*

(A) As of old, he that would be aided must seek—even as has been indicated. As has been given, let all things be done in order. Seeking, knowing—as ye measure, as ye act in thought, in mind, in heart, in body, and the imaginations of thine self become *materialized* in other's actions.

Reading 281-5

(Q) *Please give the healing group an affirmation that may be used in blessings our offerings as they are received?*

(A) *May this be used in the manner as may be directed by Him, the giver of all gifts.*

(Q) *Should we hold each individual name separately in meditation, or hold the list as a group?*

(A) This may be done either way, but it should be done in unison for the better effect. This may be alternated from time to time, even as He did. As He gave, "As ye have seen me do, do ye likewise, and greater things than I have done ye may do in my name, for I go to the Father . . . "

Reading 281-6

(Q) *[115]: Could I become a healer? If so, what method should I use?*

(A) That as seemeth to thee that channel through which an individual, or entity, may get hold of that which is being given out by self. There are, as seen, many *various* channels through which healing may come. That as of the individual contact; that as of the faith; that as of the laying on of hands; that as will create in the mind (for it is the builder in a human being) that consciousness that makes for the closer contact with the universal, or the *creative* forces, in its experience. That which is nearest akin to that concept built. Use that thou hast, then, in hand.

(Q) *Any message for the group at this time?*

(A) Be not weary in well doing. Draw nigh unto Him, He will draw nigh unto thee. We are through.

Reading 281–22

(Q) [585]: *Do I hold my healing meditations correctly?*

(A) Who should judge as to whether one or another holds correctly? Does there come that answer within that thy meditation, thy prayer, is raising within thee that answer as thou would have go to those whom thou wouldst help? Then know that these are correct, when that answer comes. If these do not always answer, meet thy Lord within. Let Him, in the still, small voice from within, guide thee. For, He is not far from thee. Thou only needest to open the door of thy consciousness, that He may enter in.

(Q) *General question: Why are we coming in contact with so many youthful mental collapses?*

(A) These conditions, as we have pointed out in those things given through these channels, are from there again and again entering this sphere of activity those that have wandered far afield. As an individual or a group, by the natural law of attraction, sets self, chooses to be a channel that may aid others, it attracts, it draws those that *need* that which may be given through such a channel. Hence the *seeming* knowledge that there is more apparent the breaking down of those in those years when there should be the strengthening for the work, the service to be done. Thou art opening the gate! Be ready with the answer. For, His promise has been, "Take no thought (if ye abide in me) when that hour comes; for it will be *given* thee what thou shouldst answer them." For, ye have been *chosen* from the foundations of the world for a service to thy fellow man, in and through Him that *made* the world. Be faithful, then. Be not unmindful of that thou may bring to pass—the *glory* of the Christ in the lives of those that are seeking—seeking!

(Q) *Any general guidance for the group?*

(A) That which has been given oft, heed ye. Let each individual study (not for his brother, but for himself) to show thyself approved unto God, that is *within* thee; rightly divining [dividing II Tim. 2:15] the words of truth, keeping self unspotted from the world. And as much as it lieth *within* thee, through the grace of God the Father, live peaceably; doubting not. For that which confronts thee is *thy* job, *thy* place, *thy* activity *fill* that place *Thou* hast in thine own surroundings! Not what others would do in greener fields, or in surroundings more materially pleasant, but make that which is about thee *shine* with the love of the Christ that gave Himself—that was abused by His own, yet gave Himself, His life, His body, that others might have an access to the Father.

We are through.

Reading 281-24

How, then, does the activity of *any* influence act upon the individual system for bringing *healing* in the wake or the consciousness, to become conscious of its desire?

When a body, separate from that one ill, then, has so attuned or raised its own vibrations sufficiently, it may—by the motion of the spoken word—awaken the activity of the emotions to such an extent as to revivify, resuscitate or to change the rotary force or influence or the atomic forces in the activity of the structural portion, or the vitale forces of a body, in such a way and manner as to set it again in motion.

Thus does spiritual or psychic influence of body upon body bring healing to *any* individual; where another body may raise that necessary influence in the hormone of the circulatory forces as to take from that within itself to revivify or resuscitate diseased, disordered or distressed conditions within a body.

For, as has been said oft, any manner in which healing comes—whether by the laying on of hands, prayer, by a look, by the application of any mechanical influence or any of those forces in materia medica—must be of such a nature as to produce that necessary within those forces about the atomic centers of a given body for it to bring resuscitating or healing.

The law, then, is compliance with the universal spiritual influence that awakens any atomic center to the necessity of its concurrent activity in relationships to other pathological forces or influences within a given body. Whether this is by spiritual forces, by any of the mechanical forces, it is of necessity one and the same. Many are the divisions or characters of those ills that befall or become a portion of each individual body. Some are set in motion so that certain portions of the glandular system or of the organs of the body perform more than their share. Hence some are thin, some are fat, some are tall, some are short.

What said He? Can anyone by taking thought make one hair white or black, or add one cubit to his stature? *Who* giveth healing, then?

It is in any manner the result only of compliance to the First Cause, and the activity of same within the individual's *relative* relation to its own evolution.

Ready for questions.

(Q) *Is group action more effective than individual, and if so why?*

(A) "Where two or three are gathered in my name, I am in the midst of them." These words were spoken by Life, Light, Immortality, and are based on a law. For, in union is strength. Why?

Because as there is oneness of purpose, oneness of desire, it becomes motivative within the active forces or influences of a body. The multiplicity of ideas may make confusion, but added cords of strength in one become of the nature as to increase the *ability* and influence in every expression of such a law.

(Q) *In any form of psychic healing, is an etheric intermediary employed?*

(A) Possible; but the etheric body of the individual seeking or finding expression must be in accord with that which draws upon such an influence.

(Q) *In certain types of insanity, is there an etheric body involved? If so, how?*

(A) Possession.

Let's for a moment use examples that may show what has oft been expressed from here:

There is the physical body, there is the mental body, there is the soul body. They are One, as the Trinity; yet these may find a manner of expression that is individual unto themselves. The body itself finds its own level in its *own* development. The mind, through anger, may make the body do that which is contrary to the better influences of same; it may make for a change in its environ, its surrounding, contrary to the laws of environment or hereditary forces that are a portion of the 'elan vitale' of each manifested body, with the spirit or the soul of the individual.

Then, through pressure upon some portion of the anatomical structure that would make for the disengaging of the natural flow of the mental body through the physical in its relationships to the soul influence, one may be dispossessed of the mind; thus ye say rightly he is "out of his mind."

Or, where there are certain types or characters of disease found in various portions of the body, there is the lack of the necessary 'vitale' for the resuscitating of the energies that carry on through brain structural forces of a given body. Thus disintegration is produced, and ye call it dementia praecox—by the very smoothing of the indentations necessary for the rotary influence or vital force of the spirit within same to find expression. Thus derangements come.

Such, then, become possessed as of hearing voices, because of their closeness to the Borderland. Many of these are termed deranged when they may have more of a closeness to the universal than one who may be standing nearby and commenting; yet they are awry when it comes to being normally balanced or healthy for their activity in a material world.

Reading 281–14

(Q) May we be given a prayer of joyousness and praise at this time?

(A) Come! Let my heart be lifted in praise and adoration of the wondrous love that the Father sheds upon the children of men. Come, let all be glad in the opportunities that are given to serve in His name day by day. Come, let us be joyous in the truth that, "inasmuch as ye did it unto the least of these my little ones, ye did it unto me." Let the love of the Son be magnified in our lives that others may know that the joyousness of service brings peace and harmony to our hearts as we serve. Come! Give thanks unto Him, for we would make our own lives, our own bodies, a dwelling place of the love that the Father would manifest unto His children. Come, give place to His Holy name, that here may come joyousness in the hearts of men at the coming of the Christ into the lives and the experiences of many.

(Q) Is there any advice to us concerning those we are holding in meditation?

(A) Not as ones that would pry into the affairs of individuals, rather as that necessary element in the experience of others in seeking, in unburdening the conditions in their experience, know more of those things that hinder and that make those that seek afraid; for in the troubled heart comes those experiences that make for doubts and fears.

Consider that even at the beck and call of the Master, and even in His presence, Peter began to sink. So we, in the weakness of the flesh, in the face of doubt and fear, often begin to sink and lose our way. So, when there is held by a group as a whole those *strengthening* influences that may make others know that, "Yea, a prayer is said," there is seeking—seeking—that the one faltering may be made strong in His might, His power. Remember, all, how thin is the veil between the sublime and the ridiculous. Make not thine self absurd or ridiculous in thine own eye, in thine neighbor's eye. Keep in the way that makes for life—everlasting.

(Q) We would appreciate a Christmas message to be sent to those we are aiding.

(A) Come! Let us make a joyous noise unto the Lord, the rock of our salvation: who in times past and in the present makes known the joyous message unto the sons of men: for there is alive this day the Christ spirit that came as upon the wings of the angels, that made known the glad tidings unto the men in that far land. He is not far away today! But in "thine own heart" may we hear that voice come to us and say, "peace—be still! It is I, fear not: for I, Thy Saviour, am with thee this day."

Reading 281-28

(Q) Are we using the correct methods of breathing and intonation in our group meditations?

(A) As has been given in Meditation, to some, *this* then is the correct manner: As has been given so oft of old, purge ye your bodies, washing them with water, putting away those things of the mind and of the body; for tomorrow the Lord would speak with thee.

Hence in this group make thy mind, thy body, as a fit subject for a visit of thy Lord, thy God. Then as ye seek *ye know,* as He hath given, that the wedding feast is prepared and thou hast bid the guests, and that ye have come with the garments of the feast with thy Lord, thy Master, thy King, thy Savior.

For lowly as He was in His earthly ministry, He honored all such that gathered for the commemoration of a union of body, a union of mind, a union of strength for their worship, their sacrifice, their meeting with their God.

So do ye in thy meditation. For thy prayer is as a supplication or a plea to thy superior; yet thy meditation is that thou art meeting on *common* ground!

Then prepare thyself!

In breathing, take into the right nostril, *strength!* Exhale through thy mouth. Intake in thy left nostril, exhaling through the right; opening the centers of thy body . . . [The readings recommended breathing in through the right nostril and out through the mouth three times, slowly and deeply, followed by three times in through the left nostril and out through the right, slowly and deeply.]

Reading 281–7

(Q) . . . *Please give us more information concerning the law of vibrations during meditation, and how we can understand and use that which we experience.*

(A) As has been given, and as experienced by many, in opening self to the unseen forces about us, yet warred ever by those influences save when in the presence of His influence, then as the forces are raised in self *know*—without doubt—there *are* His protecting influences, able, willing, capable, and *will* aid in that direction in which such vibrations, such influences, are raised to those individuals to whom they be directed, even by the spoken word; for, as is seen, as is understood by many, by most, that the *unseen* forces are the *active* forces, the *active* principles. That which *becomes* as a manifestation is that which has been acted *upon by* those unseen forces and influences. What produces same? These are the *vibrations* to which a body has raised by its attunement of its whole being, its whole inner self, of a consciousness of that divine force that emanates in Life itself in this material plane. In sending such forces out, then, be mindful that there is no doubt that these will bring that as *He* sees fit, "Not my will, O Father, but Thine be done!" What did *this* bring to Him? The cross, the burdens, the crown of thorns—yet in its essence it brought those abilities to overcome death, hell and the grave. So, as in our raising ourselves to that understanding that His presence is guiding and directing those influences about those to whom we would direct His cause (for they have called on us), then *know* His will *is being* done in the manner as *thou* hast sent same to that individual!

(Q) . . . *Please give a definition of vibration in relation to healing.*

(A) This would perhaps require several volumes to give a complete definition. Vibration is, in its simple essence or word, *raising* the Christ Consciousness in self to such an extent as it may flow *out* of self to him thou would direct it to. As, "Silver and gold I have none, but such as I have give I unto thee." "In the *name* of Jesus Christ, stand up and walk!" *That* is an illustration of vibration that heals, manifested in a material world. What flowed out of Peter and John? That as received by knowing self in its entirety, body, mind, soul, is one *with* that Creative Energy that is *life* itself!

Be not faint hearted because failure *seems* to be in thy way, or that self falters—but "how many times shall I forgive, or ask forgiveness—seven times?" "Yea, seventy *times* seven!" or, "not how I faltered, but did I seek his face again?" "Could ye not watch with me one hour?" The *man* crying out! "Sleep on, now, and take thy rest, for the hour cometh when I shall be even alone." So we find the changes, the weaknesses in the flesh—yet he that seeks shall find, and as oft as ye knock will the answer come. Seek to be one with Him, in body, in mind, in soul!

Reading 281–12

(Q) Any message for the [prayer] group as a whole?

(A) Keep in that way, in patience, in persistence, in sincerity, in truth. Faint not that there are periods when apparently little is seen to be accomplished externally. Know that thou hast set in motion that leaven that worketh all unseen, yet will bring the consciousness of His love, His hope, His presence, into the lives of all. Each should be patient first with self, in honor preferring one another. Sit not in the seat of the scornful. Stand not in the place of the cynic. Be mindful not of things of high estate; rather give place to that that makes for sweetening in the lives of all; for he that wishes his brother well, yet makes no move to aid or supply, or to comfort, or to cheer, is only fooling self. He that would know the way must be oft in prayer, joyous prayer, *knowing* He giveth life to as many as seek in sincerity to be the channel of blessing to someone; for "Inasmuch as ye did a kindness, a holy word, a clothing in act as to one of these the least of my little ones, ye have done it unto me." As He knoweth thee, so may ye know Him, ye who have been chosen for the various channels of activity in spirit, in mind, in body, for the manifesting of His glory in the earth. Be faithful. Do not allow self to be so overcome in *any* manner as to miss that calling in Him; for He is faithful who has promised to be near.

World Affairs and the Power of Prayer
TEXT OF READING 3976-23

This psychic reading given by Edgar Cayce for the Eighth
Annual Congress of the Association for Research & Enlightenment, Inc., Virginia Beach, Virginia, this 13th day of June,
1939.

PRESENT

Edgar Cayce; Gertrude Cayce, Conductor; Gladys Davis,
Steno. All those attending the Eighth Annual Congress.

READING

Time of Reading 3:30 to 4:00 P. M.

GC: You will continue the discourse begun this morning on World
Affairs which Edgar Cayce will present at the opening meeting of the
Eighth Annual Congress of the Association for Research and Enlightenment, Inc. Please comment fully on the conditions which exist in each
of the principal countries.

EC: Many will ask, "What has the foregoing to do with conditions
which exist in the various countries? What has it to do with those countries that are called democracies; or Fascism, Communism, or any of the
totalitarian countries?"

As everyone should see from that which has been indicated, it is that
there must be first the individual conviction of the need to trust God
for the needs of His people at all times and under every circumstance,
whether this is under democracy or any other form of government.

The disturbance has ever been, since the first disagreement as to
what sacrifice and as to the character of sacrifice was to be offered, that
someone is to set a rule by which all others are to be judged, or to
which all are to conform—when the *rule* is—and should ever be—that as
was proclaimed from the beginning, "Know, O Israel, the Lord thy God
is *one!*"

And while each soul seeks to manifest in a material world, the purpose, the idea—yea, the ideal is that all are to work in unison for the
good of all.

What, think ye, has caused or did cause that meeting of the democratic countries, or the democracies and the totalitarian states? Was it because of the wisdom of the men that met, or that either of the four there had their own way? Rather was it not the prayers of the mothers and the fathers of each nation represented there, that there might not be that destruction of human life which would be the natural outcome of open conflict? [Versailles Treaty?, Munich Agreement?]

It is, then, still the challenge to each country, to each nation—that while there is, to be sure, the natural instinct or purpose of self-preservation, it is to be less and less of self and more and more for that which was from the beginning.

Then, there needs be that not so much be set as to this ritual, or this form, or the other, for any given peoples or any nation, but rather that the individuals in each nation, *everywhere*, are to turn again *to* the God of the fathers and not in self-indulgence, self-aggrandizement, but more and more of self-effacement.

For as the people of each nation pray, *and* then live that prayer, so must the Spirit work.

Then—each of you here—*give god a chance* to show what great blessings He will give to those who love Him. This does not mean that ye, or *anyone*, would condone persecutions anywhere or in any form. For, know ye, His laws fail not—"As ye sow, so shall ye reap."

Man can only begin, then, within himself. And as he applies that he knows, that he understands of God, in his daily life, so may there be given him the next step to make.

Then ye ask, "What is to be the outcome of England and France in their efforts to join hands with Russia as an encirclement of the totalitarian regime?" These, so long as they are in keeping with God's purposes with man, will succeed. When they become active for self-preservation without the thought or purpose of their fellow man, they must fail.

So it is with the endeavors of Germany, Italy, Japan. As they attempt to preserve their own personalities, their own selves, without thought of their fellow man, they may succeed for the moment, but "God is not mocked," and whatsoever a man, a country, a nation sows, that it must reap.

"What then," ye ask, "is to be the outcome? What is there that I can do about it?"

Let thy daily life be free from criticism, from condemnation, from hate, from jealousy. And as ye give power to the Spirit of Peace, so may the *Prince of Peace*, the love of God, manifest.

So long as ye turn thy thoughts to the manners and means for meeting and overcoming those destructive forces, ye show forth that which may bring to the world that day of the Lord. For the promise is that in the latter days there shall be the purposes in the *hearts* of men, everywhere!

There *is* in every land today—through the prayers that have gone up for the last two years—a more seeking for that at–onement with Creative Forces, a more seeking for the knowledge and the purposes of God, than there has been for ages.

Then, rest not on those things that become as quicksand about thee, but on the true, the tried arm of God. For the earth is His, and the fulness thereof.

To each of you, then: Give God a *chance!* Know that no man is in authority or in power in the earth today save as has been granted of God, the He, the Father, may be better known. Man sees only for the moment. When man has purposed in his heart, God hath seen the end thereof.

And what is the will of the Father? That no soul should perish! And *all* will be, all *are*, tried so as by fire.

The fires of nature are what? Self–indulgence, self–glorification.

Then, turn ye—every one—to the Law of Love, and love thy neighbor as thyself.

We are through for the present.

General Thoughts on Prayer
Reading 364–10

How does prayer reach the throne of mercy or grace, or that from which it emanates? From itself! Through that of *crucifying, nullifying*, the carnal mind and opening the mental in such a manner that the Spirit of truth may flow in its psychic sense, or occult force, into the very being, that you may be one with that from which you came! Be thou faithful unto that committed into thy keeping! Life *itself* is precious! For why? It is of the Maker itself! That *is* the beginning! The psychic forces, the attunements, the developments, going *to* that! As did many in that experience. And Enoch walked with God, and he was not for God took him. As was many of those in those first years, in this land, this experience.

Reading 3498-1

First begin with prayer in self. Pray to be shown—by prayer, to be shown—whether there be the answer within self or not.

Then, through deep meditation, even leaving the body almost in same, find there the answer—through the raising of the kundaline forces in the body itself, from the cells within the Leydig gland, so as to carry energies through the body. Get the answer as to whether now, here, we would apply physical conditions for the benefit, for the correction.

Reading 1158-14

(Q) Is it correct when praying to think of God as impersonal force or energy, everywhere present; or as an intelligent listening mind, which is aware of every individual on earth and who intimately knows everyone's needs and how to meet them?

(A) Both! For He is also the energies in the finite moving in material manifestation. He is also the Infinite, with the awareness. And thus as ye attune thy own consciousness, thy own awareness, the unfoldment of the presence within beareth witness with the presence without. And as the Son gave, "I and my Father are one," then ye come to know that ye and thy Father are one, as ye abide in Him.

Thus we find the manifestations of life, the manifestations of energy, the manifestations of power that *moves* in material, are the representation, the manifestation of the Infinite God.

Yet as we look into the infinity of space and time we realize there is then that force, that influence also that is aware of the needs, and there is also that will, that choice given to the souls of men that they may be used, that they may be one, that they may apply same in their own feeble, weak ways perhaps; yet that comes to mean, comes to signify, comes to manifest in the lives of those that have lost their way, that very influence ye seek in the knowledge of God.

For until ye become as a savior, as a help to some soul that has lost hope, lost its way, ye do not fully comprehend the God within, the God without.

Reading 4028-1

For all prayer is answered. Don't tell God how to answer it. Make thy wants known to Him. Live as if ye expected them to be answered. For He has given, "What ye ask in my name, believing, that will my Father in heaven give to thee." Again it has been said, and truly, the Father will not withhold any good thing from those who love His coming . . .

(Q) *Will the prayer which I have been praying for seven years be answered?*

(A) As indicated, all prayers are answered when the individual doesn't tell God just how to answer them.

Reading 5732-1

Pray about it a lot, not merely at this time, for you may be given that which may be helpful, but apply it and seek to use thy abilities in constructive ways with thy associates.

Reading 2823-3

A good lesson here for everyone to learn who would know the way of the Lord! Be patient, be just, be kind, be longsuffering, show brotherly love—and then don't worry about what's going to happen! but be sure you do these! When you get to the place where you would worry (this is for the entity), stop and pray! For why worry, when you can pray? For God is not mocked, and He remembers thee in thy sincerity in thy purpose.

Reading 3509-1

No doubt overpowering fear. Right about face! Know it is within thee! Defying this has brought the fear, has brought the anxieties. Turn about, and pray a little oftener. Do this several weeks, yes—let a whole moon pass, or a period of a moon—28 days—and never fail to pray at two o'clock in the morning. Rise and pray—facing east! Ye will be surprised at how much peace and harmony will come into thy soul. This doesn't mean being goody-goody—it means being good for something, but let it be creative and not that which will eventually turn and rend thee.

Reading 1125-3

Let the approach be made in humbleness of heart, seeking not that as of self but as thy Lord, thy God, thy Savior would have thee do. Pray sincerely, pray earnestly, until thou hast thine answer within thine own conscience. This is the best preparation for the ordeal of kindly, gently, reasonably, meditating, agreeing, disagreeing, as to choices to pursue.

Do that. In that manner may there be no regrets. Otherwise, there will be a shortening of thy abilities to minister to others, to contribute to the welfare of thy son as well as others.

And know, "Inasmuch as ye do unto the least of thy brethren, ye do to thy *Maker.*" And thy choices must live with thee daily.

Reading 378-40

In seeking to make self, with all of the material, mental and spiritual development, in accord with divine influences and purposes, those that make their lives and activities in material or mental in accord with the laws that are manifested in the spiritual attributes seen in a material world, the application makes the growth as is spoken of; ye grow in grace, in knowledge, in understanding of the ways He would have thee go.

Not merely with lip service. Not merely with mental desire—that is born of that which is the rule or standard of application of that the mind, the body finds to do—but in truth and in the inner self crying, *"Lord, use me! Let that which Thou seest is best be done in me, through me, at this time. Let my mind, my soul, my soul body, seek in keeping with that, and those ways and channels to make known in material things to those who seek to know, those that depend upon the activities of the soul and mind of this body, that their Redeemer liveth and doeth all things well."*

Let that mind be in thee that was in Him that said, "Lord, let this cup pass from me; nevertheless, not my will but thine be done in me and through me just now."

Reading 1842-1

For He indeed stands at the door of every consciousness of man that seeks to know; and will enter if man will but open.

Let thy activity, then—whether in that capacity as the minster of the Gospel or as the minister of the gospel of the law—be in that attitude of loving and making for that intercession for the wish in the experiences of every soul that is seeking to know more of its relationships to its Maker.

Reading 1304-1

One may not pray with long prayers of thankfulness for this or that, as in the experience of others, and still hold a grudge or a feeling of animosity, or a feeling of undue consideration for other individuals at least attempting—in their own ways—to be of help, whether in a feeble way or in whatever way. For all power that is in the hands of man has been *lent*, and it is not of man's knowledge but of God.

Thus when individuals hold a grudge they are fighting the God within themselves against the God within the individual or soul for whom or towards whom such is held.

Reading 612-1

Hence, as we would give, do not change in the present; but know rather within self—and through the self—that those who wait upon, those who wait with, those that administer to this body, keep that constructive force in the minds and the hearts, that there may not be that combative force for the life forces in the body to combat in its struggle for expressions in a material world. For, it has been given, "He will give His angels charge concerning thee, lest at any time ye dash thy foot against a stone." But He will bear thee up, if ye will look to Him. Aid those in their ministrations through thy prayers for them, as well as for those things that may bring to the activity of this body the awareness of their relationships to constructive life . . .

(Q) *What can the mother do to assist the doctors?*

(A) Pray with them, aiding the body of [612] to meet those necessary emergencies in the experiences.

Reading 3569-1

Not that these are to be as worries, for remember the injunction—never worry as long as you can pray. When you can't pray—you'd better begin to worry! For then you have something to worry about! (This is for the parents—not the child!)

Reading 3976-20

And know that all stand as one before the judgement bar of the Creator.

Hence prayer, and more prayer; and as we have given, *live* toward one another as a nation, as a brother nation to the others—on *either* side—as ye pray!

Do not pray one way and live another! Be consistent, be persistent.

Reading 281-20

(Q) Is the Lord's Prayer as recorded in the Bible correct? If not, would appreciate it as was given by the Master to the disciples.

(A) This may be given, but rather should the seeker use that which *is* given—as the Lord calls on all to do. Make its purpose and its intent a portion of thine self. For, there be many misinterpretations, poor translations, but to find fault with that thou hast and not use same is to make excuses that you haven't it as it was given. Art *thou* on speaking terms with thy Lord? If not, why not? *Have* that rather that *He* would give thee, than from *any* other source!

When He gave, "As ye seek in my name, that ye may have if ye believe," than act that way. He will draw near unto thee [if thou] wilt thou draw near unto Him.

Let thy prayer be that He will ever show thee, direct thee, lead thee. [5/21/34 See also 378-44 re Lord's Prayer.]

Prayer and Spiritual Healing

Reading 1967-1

And, above all, *pray!* Those who are about the body, use, rely upon the spiritual forces. For the prayer of the righteous shall save the sick.

Know that all strength, all healing of every nature is the changing of the vibrations from within—the attuning of the divine within the living tissue of a body to Creative Energies. This alone is healing. Whether it is accomplished by the use of drugs, the knife or what not, it is the attuning of the atomic structure of the living cellular force to its spiritual heritage.

Then, in the prayer of those—live day by day in the same manner as ye pray—if ye would bring assistance and help for this body.

Reading 552–1

(Q) *Any further advice for those in charge of the body?*

(A) In that which has been indicated there is seen that there must ever be that prayerful attitude that at all times in the ministering, in the care, there may be done that which will not only make for an attitude of helpful hopefulness for the body, for the mental attributes, for the physical forces, but that there may be gained patience, kindness, brotherly love, endurance, and—most of all—consistency in the attitude in the activities of those about the body.

During the periods when massage is being given, let *this* be as the prayer:

We thank Thee for the opportunity, O Lord, that we may in some measure meet those things Thou has given for Thy children in this material world. Let the power of the Christ Spirit, through those promises given, be made manifest in my life as I minister now—and in the life of this body, [552] [EC called her [...] "Sanford" instead of her real last name in this incarnation.]—*be done that, O God, as Thou seest is best at this time.*

Reading 4058–1

Then, as the body goes to sleep, let the parents—together, not separately—give suggestions for the body. The suggestions should be for a unified activity of mind with mind, to control the subconscious and to control the activities reacting from the suggestions to the organs of the sensory system—in prayer, in meditation.

This, too, requires that the parents live that they pray for, and that the suggestions be made in unison. These words would or should be altered, to be sure, for these must be responses of those responsible for the body, from their very inner being. But these thoughts should be included:

Father, God! In Thy mercy and in Thy love, be Thou present with us now, as we seek to guide the body and mind of this Thy child in becoming a better channel of service to Thee at this time.

Then the suggestion to the child, (calling his name): thy inner self, thy subconscious self, thy super-conscious self will react to the will of the Father–God; that ye may be a better channel for His service in the earth.

These suggestions, of course, may alter from time to time, but these should be given consistently and daily. Give at least an hour each evening to this service. It will bring to the parents, it will bring to this entity, [4058], the activities for this body to be a physical, mental and spiritual manifestation of the love, of the promises given the child of men.

Reading 4013-1

GC: You will go over this body carefully, examine it thoroughly, and tell me the conditions you find at the present time; giving the cause of the existing conditions, also suggestions for help and relief of this body; answering the questions, as I ask them:

EC: Yes. We have the body here.

As we find disturbances here indicate—as they are active principles through the sensory organisms of the body and the sensory system—an incoordination between the impulses, the brain reflexes, and the spiritual forces of the body.

Thus the condition is karmic in its reaction.

Those who are responsible for the body-physical need not feel that this responsibility can be delegated to someone else, even though others may be physically better able to cope with or to train the body for its present conditions.

These disturbances might be helped if there would be the daily prayer together of those responsible for the body; not one day and then skip one, but each day for a period of three hundred sixty-five days. As the body goes to sleep let those responsible for the body-physical meet over the body, or with the body, and in prayer make suggestions to the body as it sleeps.

True this should have been begun six years ago but it still may aid.

Do not begin unless there is sincerity in both parents of this entity.

Otherwise, let others give that instruction, that help—for the body is meeting itself; but so must those responsible for this entity meet themselves.

Reading 1371-2

(Q) Is she giving her treatments correctly?

(A) These are very good, but keep persistent and the more prayerful when these are administered.

In making the suggestions as the body is losing itself in sleep or slumber, make these not for that as would be directed by the mother in that as *she* would like for the body to be, but that the body may build that purpose, may *fill* that purpose for which it entered in this experience, in the way, the manner, the directing forces of divine influence may act with the bodily forces of [1371].

Reading 1371–3

(Q) *Is she responding properly to the suggestions given by the mother at night?*

(A) There are times when there is a wonderful response. There are others when this is not so well. But be persistent and very prayerful and meditative; and we will find this will increase in its effectiveness as the adjustments are made, and as there is accomplished the alleviation of activities through the cerebrospinal and sympathetic system.

(Q) *Are these suggestions being given properly?*

(A) These are very good; only the persistence be kept—and do not let doubt and fear enter!

Hold to that which has been indicated as to the source of the assurance, the faith, the activity.

Reading 496–1

And, if the mental and spiritual forces are acted upon by those that have an interest in the welfare of the mental and spiritual reactions of this body, [496], through the power of intercession by meditation and prayer, to counteract the forces from without that are working with this body, there may be brought an awakening within—in correcting these conditions—and an awareness that there is a worth while experience for self in the activities of the entity's manifestation of life, and will bring the abilities to be active in directions that would make for a change that will not only be helpful, hopeful, but worth while . . .

(Q) *In what manner may his sister [439] help him?*

(A) By making the stronger intercession in prayer, and in getting or asking others to aid in and with her in same. For, where there is that intercession made through the combined efforts of many, the greater may be that directed influence towards the activity of any soul, any mental being.

Reading 366-5

Hence in the present we find the necessity for the ministry of others to the needs of the body, of the mind, and of those things that may surround same. Not that it is other than meeting that thou hast imposed upon thine self, but must wait rather on what *others* may do respecting that *they* know of the law or purpose of activity in material planes.

Hence, more and more must there be builded in the self in the present less and less of self, but more and more of the desire that the Giver of good and perfect gifts may use the body, the conditions, the experiences of self, as an example, as a stepping-stone in the experience of others for the knowledge of the at-oneness of universal force or creative energies in *their* activity towards others.

Then, self becoming as naught more and more will make for that which may be the prayer, the supplications, the purpose, the desire of the whole being: *Use me, Father, as Thou seest that may bring to me more and more the awareness of the fact that the saving influence from self can only be in him who gives life, light and immortality to those that would seek Him.*

And realizing that He, the Christ, has not willed that any should perish: *Use Thou me, and cleanse me from all unrighteousness, creating a new spirit within me, that the flesh and the mind may be quickened the more, for Thou art the giver, and in Thee is life. And may I praise and glory those that may aid in fulfilling those purposes Thou would have in me in the present.*

Praying for the Deceased

Reading 3954-1

Yea, pray oft for those who have passed on. This is part of thy consciousness. It is well. For, God is God of the living. Those who have passed through God's other door are oft listening, listening for the voice of those they have loved in the earth. The nearest and dearest thing they have been conscious of in earthly consciousness. And the prayers of others that are still in the earth may ascend to the throne of God, and the angel of each entity stands before the throne to make intercession.

Not as a physical throne, no; but that consciousness in which we may be so attuned that we become one with the whole in lending power and strength to each entity for whom ye speak and pray.

For, where two or three are gathered together in His name, He is in the midst of them. What meaneth this? If one be absent from the body, He is present with His Lord. What Lord? If you have been the ideal, that one to whom another would pay homage, you are then something of the channel, of the ideal. Then thy prayers direct such an one closer to that throne of love and mercy, that pool of light, yea that river of God.

Reading 281-8

(Q) *To what extent was [[5678]'s husband] helped by our prayers, mentally, physically or spiritually?*

(A) Still gaining from same!

(Q) *Can we help him further?*

(A) If he is still gaining, you can still help him!

Reading 2280-1

(Q) *Can you tell me if my older son, who passed away last May, died of natural causes or was he killed?*

(A) An accident.

(Q) *Can I be of any help to my sons now? If so, how?*

(A) Prayer for those who are seeking a way, *the* way to the light, aids ever.

As ye meditate—as ye pray—for as thy body is indeed the temple of the living God, there He hath promised to meet thee—then as ye meet Him, thy Maker, thy Lord—pray that there may be the light, the help needed, that they may be guided in that way and manner which will bring all together in the way as *He*, thy Lord, would have it.

Reading 281-15

(Q) *Please give a prayer for those who have passed on.*

(A) Father, in Thy love, Thy mercy, be Thou near those who are in—and have recently entered—the borderland. May I aid, when Thou seest that Thou canst use me.

(Q) *Is there a message for the group as a whole at this time?*

(A) Be not weary in well-doing. Faint not that there are no unusual happenings or experiences at the present. Rather know that in His own time will the glories, and the peace that comes from service, be made known from the sources that are of the greater service to Him.

Reading 3416-1

(Q) [Woman had experience feeling the presence of her deceased brother] Was there something he wanted her to know?

(A) Much that he needs of thee. Forget not to pray for and with him; not seeking to hold him but that he, too, may walk the way to the light, in and through the experience. For this is well. Those who have passed on need the prayers of those who live aright. For the prayers of those who would be righteous in spirit may save many who have erred, even in the flesh.

Reading 4938-1

GC: You will have before you the entity known as [4938], who was in one of the dormitories at Barnard College, New York City, in the early morning of Saturday, September 28th. You will tell us what you are privileged to tell, and that which will be helpful to those closely concerned. You will then answer the questions that may be asked by her aunt, present in this room.

EC: Yes, we are with the entity here.

This, as may be and should be understood by those who are interested, was an accident—and not premeditated or purposed by the entity.

The environs or surroundings that made for these happenings, in a material world, are with the entity in the present, making for better understandings.

Those that are near and dear to the entity, to make for more understandings—condemn no one, nor the circumstance. Neither mourn for those that are at rest.

There is gradually coming the awakening. This, to be sure, is an experience through which the entity, [4938] is passing in the present. It is making for a helpfulness in its understanding and comprehending of that which is the experience, the awareness of same in the present.

The body–physical that was broken is now whole in Him.

Let thy prayer then be:

"In Thy mercy, in Thy goodness, Father, keep her. Make for those understandings in my experience, in her experience, that we may draw nearer and nearer together in that oneness of purpose that His love is known more and more in the minds and the hearts of those that are in the positions of opportunities for being a channel, a messenger, in the name of the Christ. Amen."

Ready for questions.

(Q) *Is she happy, and does she understand where she is?*

(A) As given, there is the awakening, and there is the understanding coming more and more.

And soon to the Aunt may come the awareness of her presence near. These are the conditions.

(Q) *Is there anything any of us can do to help her in any way?*

(A) Let the prayer as given be held occasionally, especially in the early mornings.

We are through with this reading.

Personal Prayers

Reading 3976–26

Let thy prayer then be:

Lord, here am I! Use me in the way, in the manner thou seest fit; that I may ever be that Thou hast purposed for me to be—a light shining as in darkness to those who have lost hope, from one cause or another.

Reading 954–5

(Q) *Please give some thought or meditation as help to overcome results of the recent terrible crisis.*

(A) Just as has been given:

"O God! Not my will, not my purpose but Thine!"

Remember the prayer as He gave.

"If possible let this cup pass from me, but not my will—Thine O God be done in and through me! Here am I, Lord—use me! Though it break my body, though it purge my soul, use me and let me not abuse Thy promises but make them mine—day by day!"

Reading 1647-1

(Q) Give bedtime prayer for child suitable to bring out the best qualifications for this entity?

(A) "Lord, Thou knowest Thy children! Thou callest them by name! As we dedicate the life and the activities of the entity, [1647], to Thee, wilt Thou, O Lord, open our minds and hearts to those things that are necessary for the directing of this body and mind and soul—into those fields and activities in which the greater blessings may come to those whom this entity may serve!

"Keep him, direct him—for Thou hast promised that what we ask in His name, believing, that Thou wilt do: that Jesus, the Christ, may be glorified among the children of men."

Reading 2545-1

Let thy light so shine, day by day, that ye fail not in that standard thou hast set to thyself. Do not expect others to measure all at once. For, thou art high indeed in thy ideals. Do not lessen them, but let thy prayer be daily:

Lord, here am I—thy servant, seeking to be a greater expression of Thee among my fellow men. Show me the way, O Lord. Help me to be humble, yet glorify Thee.

Reading 1467-11

(Q) Please give me some spiritual advice. I would appreciate an affirmation.

(A) Do not at any time in thy associations with others do that thy conscience condemns thee for; that is: Let not self, nor self's purpose, be ahead of thy purpose with thy Lord. For, as ye have heard, as ye do unto the least of thy associates ye do unto thy Lord.

Let thy prayer oft be, though in thine own words:

Here am I, Lord, seeking to be a channel of help and blessings to others. Use Thou me in the way and manner thou seest fit. I acknowledge my weaknesses, but I look for the promised strength in Thee to keep me in the way I should go.

6

●

Affirmations Suggested
by the Edgar Cayce Readings

Affirmations for Meditation, Prayer, Spiritual Healing, and Personal Growth

(Note: Affirmations can be used for personal attunement and meditation; they can also be used as a focal point of concentration for the mind—building the point of focus within one's self.)

Reading 281-26

For each affirmation should, and does, fill a place, a purpose, in the minds, in the hearts, of those that—through concerted and consecrated effort—seek to be a channel and to be one with Him.

Affirmations from *A Search for God*, Books I, II & III:

BOOK I

Lesson I—Cooperation

Reading 262-3

Not my will but Thine, O Lord, be done in and through me. Let me ever be a channel of blessings, today, now, to those that I contact, in every way. Let my going in, mine coming out be in accord with that

Thou would have me do, and as the call comes, "here am I, send me, use me!"

Lesson II—Know Thyself

Reading 262-5

Father, as we seek to see and know Thy face, may we each, as individuals, and as a group, come to know ourselves, even as we are known, that we—as lights in Thee—may give the better concept of Thy spirit in this world.

Lesson III—What Is My Ideal?

Reading 262-11

God, be merciful to me! Help Thou my unbelief! Let me see in Him that Thou would have me see in my fellow man! Let me see in my brother that I see in him whom I worship!

Lesson IV—Faith

Reading 262-13

Create in me a pure heart O God! Open Thou mine heart to the faith Thou hast implanted in all that seek Thy face! Help Thou mine unbelief in my God, in my neighbor, in myself!

Lesson V—Virtue and Understanding

Reading 262-17

Let virtue and understanding be in me, for my defense is in Thee, O Lord, my Redeemer; for Thou hearest the prayer of the upright in heart.

Lesson VI—Fellowship

Reading 262-21

How excellent is thy name in the earth, O Lord! Would I have fellowship with Thee, I must show brotherly love to my fellow man. Though I come in humbleness and have aught against my brother, my prayer, my meditation, does not rise to Thee. Help thou my efforts in my approach to Thee.

Lesson VII—Patience

Reading 262–24

How gracious is Thy presence in the earth, O Lord. Be Thou the guide, that we with patience may run the race which is set before us, looking to Thee, the author, the giver of light.

Lesson VIII—The Open Door

Reading 262–27

As the Father knoweth me, so may I know the Father, through the Christ spirit, the door to the kingdom of the father. Show thou me the way.

Lesson IX—In His Presence

Reading 262–30

Our father, who art in heaven, may Thy kingdom come in earth through Thy presence in me, that the light of Thy word may shine unto those that I meet day by day. May Thy presence in my brother be such that I may glorify Thee. May I so conduct my own life that others may know Thy presence abides with me, and thus glorify Thee.

Lesson X—The Cross and the Crown

Reading 262–34

Our father, our God, as we approach that that may give us a better insight of what He bore in the cross, what His glory may be in the crown, may Thy blessings—as promised through Him—be with us as we study together in His name.

Lesson XI—The Lord Thy God Is One

Reading 262–38

As my body, mind and soul are one, Thou, O Lord, in the manifestations in the earth, in power, in might, in glory, art one. May I see in that I do, day by day, more of that realization, and manifest the more.

Lesson XII—Love

Reading 262–43

Our Father, through the love that Thou hast manifested in the world through Thy Son, the Christ, make us more aware of "God is love."

BOOK II

Lesson I—Opportunity

Reading 262-49

In seeking to magnify Thy name, Thy glory, through that Thou dost make manifest in me, O Lord, be Thou the guide, and—day by day, as the opportunity is given—let my hands, my mind, my body, do that Thou wouldst have me do as Thine own in the earth; for, as I manifest, may Thy glory become known to those through the love, the promises Thou hast made in Thy Son.

Lesson II—Day and Night

Reading 262-54

In thy mercies, O Heavenly Father, wilt Thou be the guide in the study of the manifestations of Thy love, even as in "day unto day uttereth speech and night unto night sheweth knowledge." So may the activities of my life, as a representative of Thy love, be a manifestation in the earth.

Lesson III—God, the Father, and His Manifestations in the Earth

Reading 262-57

May the desire of my heart be such that I may become more and more aware of the spirit of the Father, through the Christ, manifesting in me.

Lesson IV—Desire

Reading 262-60

Father, let Thy desires be my desires. Let my desires, God, be Thy desires, in spirit and in truth.

Lesson V—Destiny of the Mind

Reading 262-73

Lord, Thou art my dwelling place! In Thee, O Father, do I trust! Let me see in myself, in my brother, that Thou would bless in Thy son, Thy gift to me that I might know Thy ways! Thou hast promised, O Father, to

hear when Thy children call! Harken, that I may be kept in the way that
I may know the glory of Thy son as Thou hast promised in Him, that we
through Him might have access to Thee! Thou, O God, alone, can save!
Thou alone can keep my ways!

Lesson VI—Destiny of the Body
Reading 262–84

Lord, use me in whatever way or manner that my body may be as a
living example of Thy love to the brethren of our Lord.

Lesson VII—Destiny of the Soul
Reading 262–88

Lord, let me—my mind, my body, my soul—be at-one with Thee:
That I—through Thy promises in Him, Thy Son—may know Thee more
and more.

Lesson VIII—Glory
Reading 262–89

Open Thou mine eyes, O God, that I may know the glory Thou hast
prepared for me.

Lesson IX—Knowledge
Reading 262–95

Let the knowledge of the Lord so permeate my being that there is less
and less of self, more and more of God, in my dealings with my fellow
man; that the Christ may be in all, through all, in His name.

Lesson X—Wisdom
Reading 262–102

Our Father, our God, may the light of Thy wisdom, of Thy strength of
Thy power, guide—as we would apply ourselves in Thy service for others. In His name we seek.

Lesson XI—Happiness
Reading 262–106

Our Father, our God, in my own consciousness let me find happiness in the love of Thee, for the love I bear toward my fellow man. Let my life, my words, my deeds, bring the joy and happiness of the Lord in Jesus to each I meet day by day.

Lesson XII—Spirit

Reading 262-113

Father, God, in Thy mercy, in Thy love, be Thou with us now. For we know and we speak of Thy love.

And help us then to put away, for the hour, the cares of this life; that we may know in truth that the spirit and the lamb say, "come."

Let they that hear also say, "come."

Let all that will, come and drink of the water of life.

BOOK III

(Note: A Book III was planned by the original study group, and several readings were given that provided the first three affirmations. However, due to publicity about Edgar Cayce, his schedule became so filled with individuals who needed help that he was no longer able to give readings for the group.)

Lesson I—Righteousness versus Sin

Reading 262-124

Create in me, O God, a new purpose, a righteous spirit: That I may, as Thy child, be a living example of that I have professed and do profess to believe, by manifesting same among my fellow men.

Lesson II—God—Love—Man

Reading 262-129

Let that light be within me in such measures that I, as a child of God, may realize his love for man. May I live that, then, in my life day by day.

Lesson III—Man's Relationship to Man

Reading 262-130

Father, God! Let me, as Thy child, see in my fellow man the divinity I would worship in Thee.

Let me in my daily life be a witness to Him, who exemplified for

man, to man, man's relationship to God, and the manner of relationship that should be as man to man.

For we ask it in His name, Jesus the Christ.

Affirmations Suggested for Use
by the Glad Helpers' Prayer Group

**(Note: Various readings for the prayer group recommended quite a num-
ber of possible affirmations, which is why many of the reading numbers
that follow are identical.)**

Reading 281–5

*(Q) Please give the healing group an affirmation that may be used in blessing our
offerings as they are received.*
(A) May this be used in the manner as may be directed by Him, the
giver of all gifts.

Reading 281–7

There is being raised within me that Christ Consciousness that is
sufficient for every need within my body, my mind, my soul.

Reading 281–8

The love that is being expressed in my life to others through Him is
making alive in me and my loved ones!

Reading 281–10

May the Father do in me as he sees I have need of in the present—
now.

Reading 281–10

As I do, so may I expect that result in myself, in so far as it is in
accord with His will.

Reading 281–11

Use me, O Father, as Thou seest that I may best serve my fellow man.

Reading 281–11

May there be that consciousness in me that the Christ would have me have at this time, knowing that in Him all is well.

Reading 281–11

Father, Thy all healing power is manifested in life. Give Thou the awakening that this power may be manifest more and more in me, in my life day by day.

Reading 281–12

May that strength as was manifest in the consciousness of the Christ life be so magnified in me as to make every atom of my body conscious of His presence working in and through me, bringing that to pass as He sees I have need of now.

Reading 281–12

May the abundance of supply in the Christ life be so magnified in my own as to bring those conditions in my own experience that were brought to others in their consciousness of his presence in their lives, knowing that in the Father the abundance of life brings healing in my own life.

Reading 281–14

May there now be that consciousness of His presence which will bring that necessary for the awakening of the healing in my body.

Reading 281–14

May the abundance of the Christ love fill my mind, soul and body with the love that brings healing in every manner.

Reading 281–14

Be Thou merciful, O Father, in the hours of need for my body, my mind, my soul. Heal Thou my every weakness through the Christ that makes me alive in Thee.

Reading 281-14

Bring me into Thy presence, O Father, in such measures as to bring those realizations of Thy love lighting my life in its every atom, supplying that needed for making my life one with Thee in him, our elder brother, that gave that we might approach Thee the nearer.

Reading 281-15

Create within me a pure heart, O God, and renew a righteous spirit within me, that Thy love may bring that Thou seest is best for me now.

Reading 281-15

Love, as Thou lovest me, may I shed abroad to all whom I contact, that Thy goodness, Thy mercy, may abide ever with them.

Reading 281-15

In Thy righteousness, O Father, have mercy, have patience with those that seek to know Thy ways, and bless them as Thou seest now.

Reading 281-15

Keep me in the way, O Lord, that will bring healing, understanding, and a righteous heart in all my days.

Reading 281-17

Create in me, O Father, that peace, that harmony, that love, that will bring the comprehension of Thy love, Thy mercy, Thy grace, in me, in my being, just now.

Reading 281-17

As I seek, wilt Thou harken, O Father of mercy, and in the promises that were given by and through the Christ in the earth, make me whole every whit—now.

Reading 281-17

As I come to Thee, O Father, seeking to know Thy love, Thy grace, Thy power, may I see this love, this power, this mercy Thou hast promised through Thy Son, in me—just now.

Reading 281-17
Our Father, in Thy mercy help me to so live, to so keep my inner self in accord with Thy law, Thy love, as to merit these being manifested in my life, my body—just now.

Reading 281-17
Our Father, our God, in Thy manifestations of love, remember me—just now.

Reading 281-18
Create in me a righteous spirit, a correct understanding, O Lord. Aid Thou me in meeting that Thou seest is best for me through the manner of life I have lived, renewing a right spirit in me, creating a new heart and purpose in me.

Reading 281-18
As Thou, O Lord, art the giver of life, of health, make me whole through the promises we claim in Jesus, Thy Son.

Reading 281-18
As the day and the night showth forth in manifested forms the glory of the Father, so may there be made manifest in me now, through the help I seek through the Christ, my elder brother and my Lord.

Reading 281-18
Create in me that purpose that will renew the right spirit within me, bringing that Thou seest is best for me just now.

Reading 281-18
Life, love and glory are Thine, O Lord. Let these be manifested in my life as Thou seest i have need of.

Reading 281-19
May there come into my consciousness more and more the love of the Father, through the Son, day by day.

Reading 281-19

Let the words of my mouth and the meditations of my heart be such, O Lord, as to bring in my experience that Thou seest I have need of at this time.

Reading 281-19

Let Thy ways be my ways. May the desire of my heart, O Lord, be ever in keeping with Thy will. Thy will, O Lord, be done in me.

Reading 281-19

In my Father's house are many mansions. Let me so conduct my life, my ways of living, as to be in keeping with that He would have me do to become worthy of His blessings. Create in me a pure heart and renew a righteous spirit within me.

Reading 281-19

May my ways and Thy ways, O Lord, be one in the Christ-life, in the Christ-Consciousness. And may His grace, and mercy, and peace, abide with me.

Reading 281-19

Let my life be in the way thou would have it go. Let Thy love, Thy healing power, be in me: And let me ever say, "thy will be done in my life: Thou, O Lord, the guide: Thou protect me just now."

Reading 281-20

Father, fill my life, my heart, with the light of the love in the Christ, that may cleanse me from all unrighteousness.

Reading 281-20

May the desire of the heart be Thy desire, that there may be created in my experience that which will make me more aware of the Christ life in my experience.

Reading 281-20

Fill Thou, O Father, my life with peace, harmony and joy in the Christ life, the Christ Consciousness, that it may purge me and make my life as Thou would have it be.

Reading 281–20

Create in me a pure heart and renew the righteous spirit within me, cleansing my life, my heart, my body, through the love in the Christ life.

Reading 281–20

Father, Thou knowest the needs of my heart, my body. Cleanse Thou same as Thou seest it has need of, for we seek through the promises of the Christ in our lives.

Reading 281–20

Let the words of my mouth and the meditation of my heart be in the Christ Consciousness, that purgeth from all unrighteousness and maketh the body whole in His service.

Reading 281–20

Keep Thou, O Father, my ways: Directing me in the Christ way, that His promises may be fulfilled in my life.

Reading 281–21

Let me rededicate my life, my heart, my body, to the service of my God, that I may be a channel of blessing to someone, now!

Reading 281–21

Praise to the Father through His Son, the Christ, that peace and harmony is mine in my heart, my soul, now, in His name!

Reading 281–21

Father, let my life be that Thou wouldst have it be, just now. May the meditations of my heart, may the activities of my hands, be in keeping with that Thou would have me be.

Reading 281–21

Lord, our Father, our God, life and hope and faith is of Thee! Give

Thou the blessing now as Thou seest thy servant has need of.

Reading 281–21
Lord, in Thy house are many mansions. In many ways Thou makest manifest Thy love unto the children of men. Help me in my weakness to be strong in Thy might, that my body and the needs of same may be rededicated to Thy service, now.

Reading 281–21
Our Father who art in Heaven, hallowed be thy name! Praise we give to Thee for Thy loving–kindness to Thy children and to those that seek to know Thy face. Bless us all as Thou seest we have need of.

Reading 281–22
The Father that worketh in me supplieth the needs of the body, of the mind, of the soul, even as I work His ways!

Reading 281–22
Father, let Thy love, Thy mercy, Thy truth in the Christ sustain me and keep me in the way I should go!

Reading 281–22
Through the love Thou hast promised in the Savior, the Christ, I claim—O Father—those promises in Him for health, for strength for the daily needs in this material world.

Reading 281–22
As I, O God, forgive those that trespass against me, wilt Thou forgive those that do err against Thee and against me, giving them life and hope and faith!

Reading 281–22
As health and strength and sustenance flows through me in the efforts to be one with the Father, may it supply every need just now!

Reading 281-22

Let Thy ways, O Father, be my ways! Let that which Thou seest is best in my experience be mine. Keep me, O God, humble!

Reading 281-22

As the Father worketh in me, so may I also work to bring health, strength and might to my fellow man!

Reading 281-22

As the promises in the Christ are sure, so may those needs for my body, for my mind, for my soul, be safe and sure in Him!

Reading 281-23

Lord, Thou who art holy, keep and preserve Thou my every effort, that I may bring to the experience of others and to myself the awareness of thy presence abiding with them.

Reading 281-23

Let love, life and hope be the motivative forces in my thoughts and my acts day by day.

Reading 281-23

Heavenly Father, as Thou art life, so increase Thou life and love in every atom of my body as to make me one with Thee.

Reading 281-23

As Thy days, Thy ways, may be my days, my ways, wilt Thou keep thou me and those that love Thee in that way that more and more of the light of Thy love may permeate the activities of the bodies day by day.

Reading 281-23

Let love be without dissimulation. Let joy and hope pervade my life in such measures that others may take hope, may take life and know that Thou are near.

Reading 281-23

As my life is a reflection of my concept of Thou, in thy activities in the earth, O Lord, keep me in the way that I should go.

Reading 281-23

Wilt Thou, O Father, come into the lives and hearts and minds of those, as we pray for them, with them. Move Thou through the spirit of truth their expressions to enjoin in Thy love.

Reading 281-23

Father, God, keep Thou me in the way that I should go, that I may fulfil that purpose that Thou would have me fill at this time.

Reading 281-25

Lord, Thou art my dwelling place. Abide Thou, O God, in the temple of my body, that it may be wholly as Thou would have it.

Reading 281-25

Let the joy of the Lord fill my mind, my body, quickening the spirit, that the deeds that are done may be acceptable in His sight.

Reading 281-25

Lord, keep Thou my ways. Let me find joy and pleasure in manifesting such a life that it may give hope and help and cheer to others.

Reading 281-25

Lord, the maker of heaven and earth, the giver of the Christ in the hearts of men, quicken Thou the spirit within, that Thy light, Thy love, may be manifested through me.

Reading 281-25

Lord, Thou art my redeemer. In the Christ do we seek to know Thee the better. Let love and health, let joy and prosperity of the Lord quicken my ways.

Reading 281-25

Lord, Thou art the giver of all good and perfect gifts may the light of Thy countenance in Christ shine upon me now, making for the manifestations of the love Thou hast promised in Him.

Reading 281-25

Lord, maker of heaven and earth and all therein. Let the love of the Christ be my guide, that my body, my mind, may be whole in Thee: And thus be the channel of a blessing to others.

Reading 281-25

Lord, Thou art my dwelling place. Quicken the spirit within me that Thou may have Thy way with me, that I may be the greater channel of blessings to others.

Reading 281-25

. . . that as written over the door of the Temple Beautiful [Healing Temple in ancient Egypt]:

Parcoi [?] So [?] Suno [?] Cum [?]. Lord, lead Thou the way. I commit my body, my mind, to be one with Thee.

Reading 281-26

Lord, Thou art my dwelling place. Let Thy will, Thy purpose, so fill my body, my mind, that my will may be one with thee.

Reading 281-26

Lord of light, of mercy, of peace, create in me a pure heart: And renew a righteous spirit within me—now.

Reading 281-26

Our God, our Father, let my desires and the meditations of my heart, of my body, of my mind, be one with Thee: That I may be renewed and made every whit whole.

Reading 281-26

Lord, Thou art the maker of the heavens and the earth. Thou art the giver of peace and mercy and truth. Let the love that Thou hast shown in the gift of Thy Son bring that consciousness within me of my oneness with Thee.

Reading 281–26

Our Father and our God, show mercy and truth, light and justice, in my mind, in my body: That it may be renewed to a life of service for Thee in the Christ.

Reading 281–26

Let mercy and judgement, O Lord, be in my ways: That there may be a renewing of purpose, of desire, within me: In my body, in my mind: That I may be one with Thee, through the love Thou hast shown in Thy son.

Reading 281–27

May the knowledge of the Lord so fill my life, my body, as to make of me a channel in His name.

Reading 281–27

The love of God, the love of the Christ, fill my mind, my body, to a more perfect understanding, that I may be as one with Him.

Reading 281–27

Let mercy and justice and love and patience rule my mind, my body, that I may be one with the Lord.

Reading 281–27

Let Thy mind, Thy mercy, bring to me that Thou seest I have need of.

Reading 281–27

God, have mercy! God, have mercy!

Reading 281–27

Let the love of the Father make me more patient with my fellow man.

Reading 281-27
As the hart [male deer] panteth for the water, so may my heart pant for the love of the Father, as i may manifest before my fellow man.

Reading 281-27
God, the Father, Christ my elder brother, in Thee do I trust. May the love of my fellow man so fire my heart as to make me just as patient, as merciful, to those that would in error hinder my life or my experience in service to Thee.

Reading 281-28
Our Father, our God, hear the prayer of Thy servants; that we may know, that we may understand, that we may be what Thou would have us be.

Reading 281-28
Father of mercy, of love, of patience, hear Thy humble servant. Thou knowest the needs of my body, my mind, my heart. Supply from Thy bounty. For we ask in the Christ name.

Reading 281-28
Father, God, in humbleness of heart I seek. I pray Thy mercy, Thy love at this period: Not only for myself but all that seek to know Thy ways.

Reading 281-28
Father of mercy, of grace, let Thy protection be with all those that seek, in the name of the Christ.

Reading 281-28
Father, who art in heaven, blessed be thy name! May Thy love, Thy grace, Thy mercy, fill my life and make it that Thou, O God, would have it be!

Reading 281-28
Father of love, of grace and mercy, keep my feet lest they falter in Thy ways. Keep my mind and my body that they go not in the way of doubt or despair.

Reading 281–28

Father, God, in Thy Son thou hast promised that what we ask we may receive. Make my body, my mind, of such an attitude and activity as to be worthy of those promises!

Reading 281–28

Father who art in Heaven, be Thou near to those that falter, to those that are afraid. Strengthen Thou through Thy love my purposes, that I may be a light, a help, a strength to many.

Reading 281–28

Father, mercy! Mercy upon those that are wayward, that in their not understanding falter. Be patient, be kind with all!

Reading 281–35

Our Father who art in Heaven, hallowed be Thy name. Let Thy love, that has been manifested in the earth, be more and more a part of my daily life; that I may know life, health, peace and joy that are in Thee and Thy promises.

Reading 281–35

Our Father, our God. Thou art life and help and joy and peace, and only as I manifest these in my daily life may I enjoy the whole peace of the Father. Give, O Father, that peace, that joy.

Reading 281–35

Our Father, our God. As we believe in the promises of Thy Son, of thy saints, of Thy life—as manifested in me—let that life in me be perfect in thee; that the Christ may be glorified as He has promised to the earth.

Reading 281–35

Father, God, Maker of Heaven and Earth and all that in them are, I claim sonship, kinship, to Thee in Christ—Jesus—who gave that what we ask in His name may be done in my body. Give, Father, that Thou seest I have need of, now.

Reading 281-35

Let the words of my mouth, the purposes of my heart, the desires of the flesh, be attuned to the love of the Father that I may show to the sons of men.

Reading 281-35

Our Father, our God, forget not Thy promises to hear when Thy children cry unto Thee. Hear, O Father, in my weakness. Make me strong by Thy might, that I may be a living example of the love of the Father to the children of men.

Reading 281-35

Our Father, our God, let me be joyous in Thy promises. Let me be what Thou hast purposed that I should be among my fellow men: And may it be all to the glory of God, the giver of all good and perfect gifts.

Reading 281-35

Our Father who art in Heaven, hallowed by Thy name, in all the earth. Let Thy peace and Thy love heal the errors of my ways, that I may indeed claim Thy promises to the children of men.

Reading 281-35

Our Father, our God, let the light of Thy love so illumine my mind and my body that it may fulfill in the earth the purpose for which it came into being—now.

Reading 281-35

Our Father, our God, keep me in Thy remembrance even as I keep Thee and Thy love in remembrance by that I show in my life to my fellow men; that I may be a channel of help, of hope, of blessings to others.

Reading 281-35

Our Father, our God. Fill my life, my mind, my body, with the love of service to others, in such measures that my body, my mind, may be healed from that which would hinder in that great service of love for others.

Reading 281–35

Our Father, our God. Let the heaven of consciousness of the presence of the Christ light my pathway of choice: That I may choose in this life to be that for which Thy purposes brought me into being—now.

Reading 281–35

Our Father, our God. May the joy and the love of Thee so fill my life, my heart, my desires and purposes, that I may be filled with the joy and peace of the Lord—now.

Reading 281–39

Father, in Thy mercy, in Thy grace, bring to me and my consciousness the awareness of the peace of the Christ; that I may say the more and more, "Father, Thy will be done in and through me day by day."

Reading 281–39

Father of mercy and grace! Let love be the directing purpose in my life experience. Let me put away all thoughts of hatred, of lust, of only material desire; and more and more look to Thee for the hope that is set in the promises through the Christ-life.

Reading 281–39

Father, maker of heaven and earth! Thou knowest the purposes and the needs, and the desires of all. Be Thou the guide in assisting me to find peace within myself, that I may be more and more at peace with Thee.

Reading 281–39

Father of love and peace and mercy, let me realize more and more that until I have found peace with my fellow man I may not find that peace with Thee that brings the full understanding of Thy love to Thy servants here.

Reading 281–39

Father, God! We claim thy promises in Jesus, the Christ! Let me so live that His peace and His grace may be mine day by day!

Reading 281-39

Father, God! Maker of Heaven and Earth! Let me see Thy grace and Thy mercy in supplying the needs of my body, my mind, my heart, now. Not as I will but Thy will, O Father, be done in me—now.

Reading 281-39

Father-Mother God! Thou in Thy love art mindful of the children of men! Let me magnify that love in my dealings with my fellow man, in the problems that are mine day by day be Thou the guide, be Thou the hope; for there is no other!

Reading 281-39

Father, who art in Heaven! All glory, all praise to Thee for the hope, for the peace, for the love Thou hast shown to me! Let me, O God, so live in body, in mind, in such a way and manner to show to my fellow man an appreciation of that love.

Reading 281-39

Father, who art in Heaven! Bring peace and harmony into my heart! Let the troubles of the moment, of the day, be as naught in my mind. But may I fill my life and my purposes and my heart with Thy love.

Reading 281-39

Gracious Father! Hear Thou the prayer of Thy servant, that seeks to know Thy way, Thy biddings. Let me, O God, be satisfied to do and be that Thou would have me do in this experience.

Reading 281-39

Our Father, who art in Heaven, hallowed be Thy name! Let peace and mercy and judgment abide in me, that I may do those things Thou would have me do in relationships to my fellow man.

Reading 281-39

Our Father and our God! In Jesus Thou hast promised that what we ask in His name will be done in our minds and in our bodies if we but believe. Help Thou, O God, our unbelief!

Reading 281–39

Our Father and our God! Let Thy love so overshadow us that we may have naught but Thee in our minds and in our purposes! And may Thy ways be our ways! Put away from our thoughts those things that would make us afraid, and help us to boldly approach the throne of mercy and grace and ask in Jesus' name that which we ought to ask for.

Reading 281–40

Our Father our God! In Thy love, in Thy mercy, be Thou nigh unto us as we approach Thy throne seeking help and aid from the cares of every soul in this world!

Reading 281–40

Father! In Thy promises through Jesus the Christ, we rely on Thy mercy, Thy bounty. Give to me, now, that Thou seest that is best for me, that I may serve Thee better.

Reading 281–40

Our Lord, our God! Teach me to pray. Teach me to ask for that which Thou would have me be and do, and bless me in that way and manner as Jesus has promised that you would.

Reading 281–40

Our Father, our God! Help Thou my unbelief! Awaken within me that spirit of truth to seek the light as is shown in the Christ and His love. And heal Thou my body, my mind, from the fear and the lust of the flesh.

Reading 281–40

Our Lord, our God! Be merciful to me—a sinner, yet seeking grace and forgiveness in Thy sight. And let me live in such a manner that my body, my mind, may be a greater channel of blessings to others.

Reading 281–40

Our Lord, our God! Be Thou with me now! I seek to do Thy will. Show me, O Lord, the way! And may my choices in my associations of every nature be such that I may be led to bless Thee more.

Reading 281–40

Our God, who art in Heaven! Hallowed be Thy name! Shed Thou, O Father, Thy love upon me in such measures as to blot out that as would make me afraid in body and in mind. Give me today, that which is best for me. And Thy will be done ever!

Reading 281–40

Our Father, our God! We thank Thee for the giving of Thy Son, for the knowledge that has come to us of His walks among men, for His giving of His own body and blood that we might have a closer tie with Thee! Then, O Father, give me strength to live, to move and do that Thou would have me do just now.

Reading 281–40

O God! I am weak, i am unworthy—yet in Christ Thou hast promised that what we ask in His name that Ye will grant in this body. Give me life, and strength, and the ability to choose aright day by day; to do, to be the things that Thou would have me be.

Reading 281–40

Our Lord, our God! Thou art gracious unto us all! And we give thanks and praise to Thee for the wondrous love thou bestowest upon each of us. Let us then, every one, show a greater appreciation in our lives, in our dealings with our fellow men. Keep us away from the petty jealousies, the little hates and spites! And fill our hearts more with the Christ love!

Reading 281–40

Our Lord, our God! Be merciful to me, now. Strengthen my body, that it may be a channel of blessing to others for Christ's namesake!

Reading 281–40

O God of mercy and light! We give thanks to Thee for Thy Son, Jesus, the Christ—and for the promises he has made known unto us! Help us to live in such a way towards others that we may show forth that love in such a manner that others, too, may know in their hearts and minds that Jesus has a care for them!

Reading 281–45

Father, God! In Thy mercy, in try love, cast out fear, hate and malice from my own thoughts, my own purposes: That thy peace, thy love, may wholy direct my life.

Reading 281–45

Father, God! Create within me a new purpose, to do Thy will in every way and manner: That fear may be eradicated from my life, and that the peace as promised in Him may fill my consciousness.

Reading 281–45

Our Lord, our God! In the promises of the Christ, Jesus, we seek thy countenance—now: That peace and love may fill our own lives, that we may shed that light into the lives of others.

Reading 281–45

Our Lord, our God! Let peace and harmony reign within my body, my mind, my soul—for Jesus' sake.

Reading 281–45

Merciful Father! Remember me in my weakness, and make my purposes one with Thee: That all fear and doubt may be blotted out of my consciousness, and only the love and peace of love divine reign within my life.

Reading 281–45

Father, God! Hear me, in my humble prayer. Take away fear and doubt: That my body may be whole: That my mind may be clear: That my soul may be at peace with Thee. This I ask in Jesus' name.

Reading 281–45

My Lord, my God! Be merciful to me! Keep fear, and doubt, and hate, out of my life. Let me fill my body, my mind, my soul, with the consciousness of the Christ-love, the Christ-peace, the Christ-harmony.

Reading 281-45

Our Lord, our God! Hear, while we pray together: That hate, and fear, and doubt, may be taken out of our lives: That love and harmony and peace may reign within our bodies, our minds, our souls—for Jesus' sake!

Reading 281-50

Holy Father, God! In Thy love, in Thy mercy, be near unto us now, as we seek comfort, guidance, direction in Thee, through our seeking to know Thy way! Bless us as Thou seest we have need of, for the Christ's sake.

Reading 281-50

Our Father, our God! As Thou hast promised in Jesus, the Christ, to be near always, hear Thou our humble prayer. Make us in the way Thou seest is best for us today.

Reading 281-50

Gracious Father! Mercy and peace be with those who seek through our humble efforts to draw near to Thee. Hear, O God, and answer: That we faint not under trial or suffering.

Reading 281-50

Our Father, our God! Hear us while we pray for those who like ourselves have forgotten the benefits in Thee. Give us more love, more peace, more ability to bring into the lives of others that which will make them aware of Thee. We ask it, Father, in the name of the Christ.

Reading 281-50

O Lord! How great is Thy love and Thy mercy to those who seek peace, and love, in Thee! Help us to realize Thy nearness: That all may come, does come, from Thee. We ask it in His name, who taught us to pray in His name.

Reading 281–50

Gracious, merciful Father! Hear our feeble efforts to approach the throne of grace and mercy, as was shown in the life of the Master, Jesus, in the earth! Let my purposes, our purposes, be in Thee, through Him—who has promised to answer when we call.

Reading 281–50

Our Father, our God! Hear us now. Be not far from us. Comfort us in our distresses of every nature. Give us of peace and love: That our bodies, our minds, may be the greater channel to manifest that love Jesus showed in the earth.

Reading 281–56

Lord, Thou art holy! Make Thou me glad; that I may bring peace and harmony in my own body, my own mind, my own purpose—just now!

Reading 281–56

Our Maker, our God! We give thanks to Thee for Thy purpose with me. Then use Thou me, O Lord, to be a light, a help to others. In His name we ask it.

Reading 281–56

Our Father, our God! We give thanks for Thy holy word, for Thy promise to man, for Thy thought of man. May I as an individual, then, give thought to others in such a purposeful way as to be a helpful influence to all I meet day by day.

Reading 281–56

Our Lord, our God! We give thanks for Thy love that is manifested in the Christ–Consciousness. Thou knowest my needs, O Lord; in body, in mind, in purse. All comes from Thee. This we acknowledge. Help Thou me, O Lord, in such measures that I may be worthy of Thy grace, and in the use of Thy purposes in the earth just now.

Reading 281–56

Our Lord, our God! I come giving thanks for the privilege of lifting my voice, my heart, my purposes to Thee. Hear Thou, O Lord, and answer in such measures that I may know Thou hast heard my humble prayer. Give that Thou seest I have need of just now. Help Thou me, O God, to be friendly to the friendless; to give love to those who have lost hope; to bring a word of cheer to those who have become discouraged for whatever reason it may be. Help me, O God, to be a channel of blessing to someone—now.

Reading 281–56

Our Father, our God! We come in humbleness yet bold to ask Thy grace and Thy mercy. For Thou hast promised that if I will but be Thy child, Thou wilt be my God. Hear, O Father, and answer in such a way that I—too—may feel that the spirit of truth has not departed from the earth. Give contentment, O Lord, in peace now. O God, give that love which I may shed—yea, may share with others—in the Christ name.

Reading 281–56

Our Father who art in Heaven, hallowed be Thy name! Thy love, O God, has kept this world in place. There is much that each of us must do, as a group and as individuals. May we be willing, O God! May we follow where Thou leadest; that we may bring again to the hearts of many that love light which makes for peace and harmony in body, in mind, in soul. We ask it in His name.

Reading 281–62

Our Father, God! As the master, the Christ, has taught us to pray, may we come at this time in that spirit seeking Thy face. May we each as individuals, and as a group of helpers, so present those promises of the Christ as to be channels of help to others.

Reading 281–62

Our Father, our God! In Thy mercy, in Thy love, be Thou near to each of this group of Glad Helpers, as we come beseeching Thee to remember those of our friends and our brothers in their distress everywhere! And especially—(and name each individual ye have on the list for that period, during that whole day or whole month); that they may be in that light, that consciousness, that we may help others to glorify Thee.

Reading 281–62

Our Father, who art in Heaven! Thou hast been gracious unto us, and for this we give eternal thanks. Yet in these periods of trial, of anxieties for our loved ones and our friends, be Thou very near unto each of us; that we may indeed enjoy that peace promised in the Christ Jesus.

Reading 281–62

Our Father, our God! As Jesus has taught us to seek Thy face in his name, wilt Thou so attune the hearts of each and every member of the prayer group seeking help through this channel, to such an awareness that they may indeed walk and talk with Him day by day.

Reading 281–62

Our Father, our God! As Thou hast heard the prayers of those, as Thou hast promised that if we would call Thou would hear, be Thou close to each and every member of this group, as well as those who seek that this group pray for them; that there may come into the consciousness of each individual the closeness of the Christ life, the Christ Consciousness, and bring His peace He has promised into the life of each.

Reading 281–62

Our Father who art in Heaven! Let that knowledge which was manifest in the Christ Jesus be of such a light in the life of each one of this group that seeks through same for strength and peace, and the mental and spiritual life, that each may so live same as to bring those material things Thou seest are best for each.

Thy will, O God, be done by each member of this group, even as I— (and call thine own name) would serve Thee.

Reading 281–64

Our Father, our God! In Thy love be Thou near to me now, as I seek the face of Jesus the Christ; who promised "that Thou shalt ask in my name will be done, that the Father may be glorified in me." Help Thou, O God, my unbelief. For I seek Thy grace, Thy mercy just now.

Reading 281-64

Our Father who art in Heaven, hallowed be Thy name! Though we are beset with disturbances on every hand, we believe that in Thee we may find peace and grace and strength. Help me to meet my problems, of every nature, in Thee: For Thou art the giver of all good and perfect gifts. Heal Thou me in Thine own mercy and strength, as is promised in Jesus the Christ.

Reading 281-64

O God, help Thou my unbelief! I realize my weaknesses and my faults, yet in Thee, and by faith in the Christ, I may find the strength to meet the joys and the sorrows of this material life. Help, O Father! In His name I ask it.

Reading 281-64

Our Father, who art in Heaven! Hallowed be Thy name. May I as Thy child have a part in the coming of the kingdom of Christ in the earth now. May I so live that His love may be manifested in those I meet day by day. May I walk, O Father, closer to Him day by day.

Reading 281-64

Our Father, our God! We thank Thee for the gift of Thy son, the Christ, in whose name we ask pardon and grace, and mercy—for the shortcomings of myself and others. Let me so live in the light of His love as He manifested in the earth. And may I be humble, may I be patient, may I be gracious: Forgiving even as I ask forgiveness for myself.

Reading 281-64

Our Father, our God! In Thy love I seek the promises made by Jesus, Thy Son. May I find health, strength, and the might to be a channel of blessing to others for His name's sake. Thou knowest my every need. Supply, O God, from Thy bounty, and in Thy love—for His sake.

Reading 281-64

Our Father who art in Heaven, hallowed be Thy name. Thy kingdom come in earth, and may I be a channel through whom this kingdom of the Christ may be the ruling force in the earth. Give, O Father, that love, that mercy which will make me strong in the way, that will enable me to be a light to others. For His name and for His sake we ask this, O God.

Reading 281–64

O Father, O God! Though I be tried seemingly beyond that I am able to bear, wilt Thou be with me—now. Help me to meet each problem, help me to meet others in such a way as to be a living example of the promises made to man through the Christ, that where and when we seek in His name, Thou wilt hear and answer speedily.

Reading 281–64

Our Father who art in Heaven, and who gave the children of men the gift of the Christ, who came into the earth that we through Him might know Thee. And as He offered Himself, His body as the sacrifice for me, O God let me so live that it will not be in vain for me to ask, and to seek, at the throne of mercy, in His name. May I so live that He, the Christ, will not deny me before Thy throne.

Reading 281–65

Father, God, bring Thou thy peace as manifested in the life of the Christ, Jesus that I, as an individual, may know thee better and in body, in mind, in purpose be nearer to Thee.

Reading 281–65

Our Father who art in Heaven, as we give thanks for Thy mercy, bring that peace that we, as individuals, may manifest the love as Christ did and does manifest to those who seek His ways.

Reading 281–65

Our Father, and our God, in the name of the Christ we seek Thy presence, Thy peace. Put away from our hearts and minds all doubts, all fears, all hates, all jealousies, that my body may be a better channel of blessings in Christ's name.

Reading 281–65

Our Father and our God, remember us in our weakness. Make us strong by Thy might, bring peace first in self, that we may live the Christ-Spirit, and peace in our hearts day by day.

Reading 281–65

Our Father, our God, in the name of the Christ, Jesus, we ask that Thou purify our hearts and our minds that the peace as manifest in the Christ may be manifest through the thoughts and the deeds done in my body.

Reading 281–65

Our Father, our God, we give thanks to Thee for Thy love and Thy mercy, and we ask that Thou would give to me, as I seek Thy purpose, that peace with my fellow man as may manifest the love of the Christ in me. Let me be the channel of warning others as to the needs of seeking Thy presence.

Reading 281–65

Our Father who art in Heaven, as we come seeking peace and harmony let us know that we will only find same as we manifest that peace in our own hearts and minds and bodies, and that as we do the biddings of the Christ we may find ourselves in His presence. Pour out Thy spirit of love, that we may do this in Thy name.

Reading 281–65

Our Father and our God, though we be troubled in body and in mind, may we realize that only as peace comes to our souls and our minds may we find relief from the turmoils of material life. Let us seek, then, Thy presence, in faith. Help, O God, our unbelief!

Reading 281–65

Our Father who art in Heaven, hallowed be Thy name! Bring mercy and love into our hearts. May we put away those little petty jealousies which may separate us from the love of God, and find peace and harmony in our attempt to be a channel of blessings to others.

Personal Affirmations, Meditations, and Prayers
Reading 412-7

(Q) *Please give me my prayer.*

(A) Each soul should seek rather that which is the answer in self, yet this may guide in the present:

Father, the giver of all good and perfect gifts, surround Thou me in my seeking to know what Thou would have me do with the consciousness of the promises made in Thy Son, that He will abide with those that seek to do His biddings.

Show Thou me the way, as I pray.

Then the way is opened before thee, either in the music that may be made by self upon the violin, or in the prostrating of self, in holding the attunement of the consciousness that may come from within, harken to that given.

If the success is not found in the first, then seek again and again *at the same period* (that may be chosen); either early in the morning or in the noonday or in the evening, whenever chosen to give that time to His making aware in thee that thou shouldst do.

For, He has ever promised; and He is faithful to those that cry unto Him in the night or in the day. For, He will not leave thy soul desolate; neither will He allow thee to be burdened beyond that thou art able to bear. But he whom the Lord loveth, he purgeth every one; that each soul may be the purer, in the light.

Reading 256-4

(Q) *Please give a personal meditation which will aid in my development.*

(A) *How gracious, O Lord, are Thy promises to Him who seeks Thy presence, even as I would become a channel of blessing to my brothers. Be Thou the guide, that I may realize Thy presence more and more, through Him that gave the promise I would not be left alone but His spirit would be with me, and my guide day by day.*

(Q) *Please give the best time length and period to hold this.*

(A) Early in the mornings and as the day goes to rest. The periods, or length, that as the *spirit* shall show thee day by day.

Reading 2369-1

(Q) *Please give me an affirmation.*

(A) *May my going in, my coming out, be wholly acceptable in Thy sight, my Lord, my Redeemer! Not my will but Thine be done in and through me. And may I so live my own life that others may be influenced to glorify Thee.*

Reading 555-11

(Q) Please give an affirmation that will help me?
(A) Let the body, the mind, be so in accord with the divine, that may find expression through me, that there may come into my experience and my associations with my fellow man that which is in keeping with that purpose Thou, O Lord, hast for me to do!
   In the name of the Son, I seek!

Reading 867-1

   Through the power of the creative forces that manifest themselves in my life, may there be brought to my experience that which the divine has purposed in my expression or manifestation at this time.

Reading 711-4

   Concerning the mental attitude: Keep in the correct spiritual influence. Let thy meditation and prayer oft be, but in thine own words:
   Lord, make me a channel of blessings to others, through Thy grace, Thy mercy, Thy love, as manifested in Jesus, the Christ. Let me in my mind and body be always in keeping with Thy purposes with the children of men.

Reading 462-8

(Q) What affirmation should I use to help coordinate myself and the Forces to obtain my desire?
(A) Let my desire and my needs be in Thy hands, Thou maker, Creator of the Universe and all the forces and powers therein! And may I conform my attitude, my purpose, my desire, to that Thou hast as an activity for me. And leave it with Him, and go to work!

Reading 2175-6

(Q) Please suggest affirmation well to be kept at this time.
(A) O Lord, our strength and our Redeemer! In the Christ-Consciousness I come to Thee, as Thy handmaid, seeking thy promises and Thy directions. Use me, O God, in such manners and in such ways that my life may reflect the love Thou hast shown to the children of men in the Christ-life. And may I ever be a channel of blessing to others.

Reading 1532–1

(Q) *Please give me an affirmation to use in meditation.*

(A) *Create, O Father, within me a pure heart! Renew the righteous purpose, the righteous desires within me—continually.*

Let me each day so live that I may constrain those that I meet day by day to glorify Thee.

Let my purposes and my desires, as in relationships to material things, as in relationships to the social activities, be such as to be to the glory of Thee—through Him who blesses all that seek through His name to know Thee!

Let my going in and my coming out be in keeping with Thy purposes with me. Let thy will, O Father, be done in me, through me, day by day.

Reading 1268–2

. . . *during those meditative periods let that thought permeate those expressions of self:*

O Lord, let me be willing to be used as thou seest I may for the fulfilling of that— O God—Thou would have me do, and be, in this experience. Thy will, O Father, not mine, be done in and through me!

Reading 2051–5

(Q) *Please suggest an affirmation to be helpful.*

(A) *Lord, here am I. Use Thou me in that way and manner that I may be a better channel of service to Thee, and for bringing grace and mercy to those I meet day by day.*

Reading 984–3

(Q) *Please give an affirmation for the mental and physical body.*

(A) *Let there be in me, O God, that purpose, that attitude, which is in accord with Thy will and Thy purpose for me in this experience.*

Let me so conduct my own life, my own activities among my associates, in a way and manner that is pleasing to Thee.

Let me be a channel of blessings to others, for Thy name's sake.

In the name of Him who has promised to be ever with me, I ask—Jesus the Christ.

A.R.E. Press

Edgar Cayce (1877-1945) founded the non-profit Association for Research and Enlightenment (A.R.E.) in 1931 to explore spirituality, holistic health, intuition, dream interpretation, psychic development, reincarnation, and ancient mysteries—all subjects that frequently came up in the more than 14,000 documented psychic readings given by Cayce.

Edgar Cayce's A.R.E. provides individuals from all walks of life and a variety of religious backgrounds with tools for personal transformation and healing at all levels—body, mind, and spirit.

A.R.E. Press has been publishing since 1931 as well, with the mission of furthering the work of A.R.E. by publishing books, DVDs, and CDs in support of its organization's goal of helping people to change their lives for the better physically, mentally, and spiritually.

In 2009, A.R.E. Press launched its second imprint, 4th Dimension Press, when A.R.E. Press features topics directly related to the work of Edgar Cayce and that includes excerpts from the Cayce readings. 4th Dimension Press allows us to take our publishing efforts further with books that are related and compatible explorations into the mysteries of life and spirituality of our existence without the direct reference to Cayce-specific content.

A.R.E. Press/4th Dimension Press
215 67th Street
Virginia Beach, VA 23451

Learn more at EdgarCayce.org or ARECatalog.com to browse our complete listing of titles.